P9-CAN-050

The Perfect Arkansas Lawn

Attaining and Maintaining the Lawn You Want

Steve Dobbs

Foreword by Janet Carson

COOL SPRINGS PRESS

Nashville, Tennessee
A Division of Thomas Nelson, Inc.
www.ThomasNelson.com

Dedication

In loving memory of my dad:

ORVILLE HAROLD DOBBS
JULY 4, 1928–MARCH 5, 1992

Memories grow more precious still when loved ones have to part,
and remain forever blooming in the gardens of the heart.
                                                  —author unknown

Acknowledgements

I learned at a young age the responsibility and work associated with lawn care thanks to my parents. I'm convinced these early obligations helped set the stage for knowing how to deal with future life endeavors. My first introduction to lawn care was by using a push mower on a 1-1^1/$_2$ acre lawn that was mostly sloped. It wasn't until I went off to college that my dad invested in a riding lawn mower—for him of course.

I would have never thought I would be back living in the same house taking care of the same lawn some 20 years later with MY family.

And wouldn't you know that a different riding mower that I inherited from my dad cut its last blade of grass during the writing of this book. So I'm grateful to all of the homeowners who will buy this book to help me purchase a NEW riding mower (grin).

I'm especially indebted to my wife Jo Alice for her support through book number two. Of course this time around there were our two young children, Ashlyn and Mason, to make the writing process much more interesting to say the least. I can't wait until you guys are old enough to mow the lawn!

Thanks, too, to the many baby sitters who allowed me time to get away to gather my thoughts for the task at hand!

And lastly, I'm very appreciative of the support and opportunities to work with the great folks at Cool Springs Press.

Happy Mowing!

The Perfect Arkansas Lawn

Published by Cool Springs Press, a Division of Thomas Nelson, Inc.,
P.O. Box 141000, Nashville, Tennessee, 37214.

Dobbs, Steve, 1959-
    The perfect Arkansas lawn / Steve Dobbs.
        p. cm.
    Includes bibliographical references (p.) and index.
    ISBN 1-930604-41-6 (pbk. : alk. paper)
    1. Lawns—Arkansas. 2. Turfgrasses—Arkansas. I. Title.
SB433 .D662 2002
635.9'647'09767—dc21

                                2002007347

First printing 2002
Printed in the United States of America
10 9 8 7 6 5 4 3 2 1

Managing Editor: Jenny Andrews
Horticulture Editor: Clint Waltz
Copyeditor: Mary Morgan
Designer: Bill Kersey
Production Artists: Bill Kersey and S.E. Anderson

On the cover: (top) Bermudagrass Close-up, photographed by Lorenzo Gunn
                (bottom) 'Tifgreen' Bermudagrass Lawn, photographed by Thomas Eltzroth

Visit the Thomas Nelson website at www.ThomasNelson.com

Contents

Foreword

If you looked at my lawn right now, you would be wondering why I am writing the foreword to a book on lawn care. I should be reading and applying the information, not telling you about a book.

A pretty lawn doesn't just happen by itself—it takes some effort on your part. You need to water, mow, fertilize, and pay attention to weeds—although, as I often say, one man's weeds are another man's wildflowers! It doesn't make a lot of sense to devote tons of time developing gorgeous flower gardens and shrub displays, and then ignore the lawn. The lawn is like the picture frame of a beautiful piece of art—you need to display your gardens in the best possible setting, and a pretty lawn can do just that.

Knowing what is needed and when to do it, can be confusing. There are hundreds of gardening and self-help books on the subject, but it is hard to have a garden book that is applicable in all 50 states. We all have regional differences with our weather, soil types, and species of grass we grow. Not many Northern horticulture writers understand what summer heat and humidity is all about.

To the rescue is *The Perfect Arkansas Lawn*, by Steve Dobbs. While Steve is a resident of Oklahoma, he works in Arkansas and has been a long time supporter of our horticultural efforts in the state. He is very familiar with hot, dry summers, and he knows what it takes to make a lawn thrive. This book will give you practical information in an easy-to-read format, and provide you with all the answers to creating a pretty lawn.

Not only is the book geared to Southern states, including Arkansas, it goes a step further and considers the three different grass growing zones we have within the state. Arkansas is a transition state, and we often struggle to maintain a beautiful lawn. Whether you want a picture perfect lawn, or one that is green and mostly weed free, Steve has the solution for you.

Janet Carson
Extension Horticulture Specialist,
University of Arkansas Cooperative Extension Service

Regional Differences

The geographic and climatic conditions in Arkansas are about as diverse as the number of turfgrass species that will thrive in the state. You'll find uniquely different soils, altitudes, rainfall, and temperatures, from Fayetteville to Pine Bluff, and Texarkana to Blytheville. As a result there are limits to what grows where.

Arkansas is divided into five land regions: the Ozark Mountains, Arkansas Valley, and Ouachita Mountains are together called the Highlands; the Mississippi Alluvial Plain, and West Gulf Coastal Plain are called the Lowlands. There is also a long, thin strip of elevated land in the northeast part of the state, in the Alluvial Plain, called Crowley's Ridge. The landscape of Arkansas varies from rugged hills, to rich floodplains, to pine forests. Different grasses will perform better in different situations, which is why matching the appropriate lawn grass to its preferred growing conditions and region is time well spent.

Turfgrass experts surmise that not much has changed over the years as far as turfgrass prominence and lawn size. What has changed, though, are the introduction of improved cultivars, and the techniques and tools with which to maintain a lawn in an environmentally safe manner.

There are six species and numerous cultivars of turfgrass that can make showy and functional lawns in the various regions of the state. The state turfgrass growing regions map will give you an idea which types of grasses will perform best in your area. The map divides Arkansas into three regions. Only carpetgrass is not recommended for Arkansas, since it prefers regions farther south.

Soils

Arkansas has at least five basic types of soil—alluvial soil in the Delta region, silt and loess (buff-colored soil deposited by the wind) on Crowley's Ridge, sandy loam in the Coastal Plain, shale and sandstone in the Ouachita Mountains, and limestone-based soil in the Ozarks. The structure of your soil has a lot to do with what will grow there. Determining the texture (percentages of sand, silt, and clay) can tell you whether or not you need to add amendments, how much watering you will have to do, and other maintenance considerations. A simple home test is described in the chapter on watering.

Whether your soil is acid or alkaline, sour or sweet, also affects what you can grow. The measurement of this is called the soil's pH. It's a good idea to have your soil tested by a local Extension Service before beginning any gardening project.

Hardiness

A cold hardiness zone is defined by the northernmost boundary in which plants can grow when the weather is at its coldest. In Arkansas these zones vary north to south, from 6a to 8a. The majority of the state is Zone 7, with coldest temperatures ranging from 10 to 0° F. The northern part of the state falls within Zone 6, with lows from 0 to -10° F. The range for Zone 8a, in the southern part of Arkansas, has temperatures somewhat less chilly, from 15 to 10° F. Some grasses are more cold-tender than others and it is important to know which hardiness zone you're in when selecting a grass for your lawn.

Many plants, lawn grasses included, are affected not only by average temperatures, but also by the range of extremes experienced throughout the year. So, in addition to cold, another temperature factor is heat, especially when coupled with humidity. If the cold of winter doesn't kill something, sometimes the heat of summer will. And much of Arkansas is certainly hot.

Lawn grasses are divided into warm- and cool-season types. The Southern States Grass Zones map shows you how the area from Texas to the East Coast is divided. A line has been drawn that bisects the southern quadrant of the U.S. North of the line is a transition zone where both cool- and warm-season grasses will grow. South of the line is the region where warm-season grasses should be used. Of course, north of the transition zone, not shown on the map, is where cool-season grasses are best.

Arkansas is divided almost in half into northern and southern sections. Some grasses will grow anywhere in the state (bermudagrass and zoysiagrass), but others are more particular. St. Augustinegrass is a warm-season grass best suited to the southern part of the state. Kentucky bluegrass and fescue are cool-season grasses that prefer the northern region.

Precipitation

One of the most obvious factors in gardening is rainfall. It can determine what will thrive in your area and how much supplemental watering you may have to do. As seen on the precipitation map, Arkansas has generally less rain in the north and more rain in the south. The highest precipitation is in the Ouachita Mountains. Rainfall for the state ranges from about 45 inches to over 60 inches per year.

Not only is it important to know how much rain an area receives over the course of the year, but also when that rain falls. In Arkansas the rain can be quite seasonal, and which season it falls is dependent on where you live. The Ozarks receive fairly consistent rainfall in the late spring and early summer. The Coastal Plain region in the southeastern half of the state can have high rainfall in late April. In different regions dry spells can occur in fall or winter or mid-summer. Situated as it is between the Southeast and the Midwest, Arkansas weather is influenced by factors coming from several directions, from cold fronts dropping down from the northwest, to hurricane activity in the Gulf of Mexico.

Knowing how much rain your area receives annually, when the rainy seasons are, and which months are the driest, will tell you when you need to be the most conscious of possible water needs in your yard. If you live in parts of the state that receive less annual precipitation, you are more likely to be a candidate for installing irrigation, or at least setting the sprinkler out during the driest times. And droughts can occur anywhere in the state. Know what to expect in your region and keep an eye on your lawn, especially if it is new. The grass will tell you when it needs water, but it's good to have some idea ahead of time when that might occur.

Maintenance

To have a beautiful lawn, you need to take good care of it, and that means maintenance. Most homeowners already know that lawns can require watering, fertilizing, and weed control, and they probably suspect there are other things they need to do as well. The Arkansas Turf Maintenance at a Glance chart in the Introduction shows you what to do and when. All of the subjects are covered more in-depth later in the book, but this offers a handy way to make a quick reference. Having a schedule can make the task at hand seem easier, and can take away the sense of panic you feel when you think you've forgotten to do something. Any aspect of gardening is seasonal, dependent on both the weather and the growth cycle of plants, and timing is everything.

Introduction

Having a healthy, green lawn is well worth the effort. Whether you use it as a practice soccer field, a complement to your flower beds, or a place to relax at the end of a long day, once it's established, and once you're familiar with the routine that will keep it at its best, a lawn can offer years of enjoyment. Don't fight the lawn—learn how to work with it.

For More Information

If you have questions about turfgrasses, lawn diseases, insects, soils, and maintenance issues, contact your state or local Extension Service office. The Extension Service is a government funded information service, organized by state and county, which anyone can use. Much of their information is free, though there can be fees for some things, such as soil tests. A web site from the U.S. Department of Agriculture (www.reeusda.gov) provides links to state and county offices for every state, and can guide you to Extension resources in your region. There are also a number of helpful publications and web sites related to turfgrass, weather, geology, and ecology. Learn more about lawns and your regional conditions so that you can get the most out of your gardening experience.

University of Arkansas
Division of Agriculture
Cooperative Extension Service
2301 S. University Ave.
Little Rock, AR 72204
(501) 671-2000
www.uaex.edu

Bermuda	**Bermuda**	**Bermuda**	**Not recommended**
Fescue	Centipede	Centipede	Carpet
Kentucky Bluegrass	Fescue	St. Augustine	
Zoysia	Zoysia	(southern counties)	
		Zoysia	

These regions indicate the areas where the turfgrasses are best adapted.
Overlapping can occur across regions depending on USDA cold hardiness zones, microclimates created by buildings and windbreaks, soil type, and annual rainfall.

USDA Cold Hardiness Zones

ZONE	Avg. Min. Temp. (°F)
6a	-5 to -10
6b	0 to -5
7a	5 to 0
7b	10 to 5
8a	15 to 10

Total Annual Precipitation

Inches

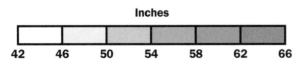

| 42 | 46 | 50 | 54 | 58 | 62 | 66 |

Source: Southeastern Regional Climate Center

13

	Jan	Feb	March	April	
Establishment *(planting, renovation, or reseeding)*					
Mowing					
Low Maintenance Fertilization					
Watering					
Aeration			if needed for compaction		
Soil Test					
Insect/Disease Management					
Pre-emergence Herbicide Warm Season Weeds			**if needed		
Post-emergent Herbicide Warm Season Weeds					
Pre-emergent Herbicide Cool Season Weeds					
Post-emergent Herbicide Cool Season Weeds		2nd application if needed			

(left label: Warm Season Grasses)

˙rate includes rainfall; higher amount in heat of summer

˝earlier pre-emergent applications may be needed as much as 2-4 weeks in southernmost counties or with early warm spells.

(Herbicides should be a last resort. Proper care is the best weed prevention. Make sure herbicide is labeled for your turfgrass

	Jan	Feb	March	April	
Establishment *(planting, renovation, or reseeding)*					
Mowing					
Low Maintenance Fertilization					
Watering					
Aeration					
Soil Test					
Insect/Disease Management					
Pre-emergence Herbicide Warm Season Weeds			** if needed		
Post-emergent Herbicide Warm Season Weeds					
Pre-emergent Herbicide Cool Season Weeds					
Post-emergent Herbicide Cool Season Weeds		2nd application if needed			

(left label: Cool Season Grasses)

˙rate includes rainfall; higher amount in heat of summer

˝earlier pre-emergent applications may be needed as much as 2-4 weeks in southernmost counties or with early warm spells.

(Herbicides should be a last resort. Proper care is the best weed prevention. Make sure herbicide is labeled for your turfgrass

May	June	July	August	Sept	Oct	Nov	Dec
raise height into late summer and fall							
*1 inch per week depending on drought conditions							
anytime - every couple of years							
watch for subtle changes and investigate							
	if needed						
					if needed		
					1st application, if needed		

and the weeds to be controlled. Follow all directions.)

May	June	July	August	Sept	Oct	Nov	Dec
					ideal		
higher in summer heat							
*1 inch per week depending on drought conditions							
anytime - every couple of years							
watch for subtle changes and investigate							
	if needed						
					if needed		
					1st application, if needed		

and the weeds to be controlled. Follow all directions.)

Southern States Grass Zones

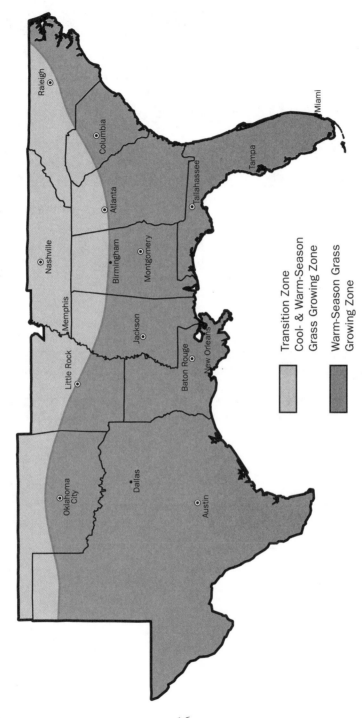

Raleigh
Columbia
Miami
Tampa
Tallahassee
Atlanta
Nashville
Birmingham
Montgomery
Memphis
Jackson
Little Rock
Baton Rouge
New Orleans
Oklahoma City
Dallas
Austin

Transition Zone
Cool- & Warm-Season
Grass Growing Zone

Warm-Season Grass
Growing Zone

Planning and Starting a New Lawn

Chapter One

Survey the Site

Test the Soil

Observe Shading Patterns

Avoid Combining Cool- and Warm-Season Grasses

Kill Existing Vegetation

Prepare the Planting Bed

Choose Among Seed, Sprig, Plug, and Sod

Water New Plantings Regularly

Site Survey

Lawns and landscapes are, unfortunately, an afterthought for many building contractors and even many homeowners. Heavy clay and other aggregate materials are often hauled in and packed down to prepare for the structure's foundation. There also may be leftover piles of sand, burned debris, roofing materials, limestone, concrete, wire, nails, and sack lunches. Grass is tough, but it is asking a lot for any plant to grow and thrive in such conditions. Dig a few holes in the area you want to plant, and see what you find. If the soil is full of debris or so compacted it is difficult to penetrate, you have a few problems to correct.

Removing compacted fill and debris in the lawn and landscape area, then bringing in good topsoil, is the best approach if at all possible. Garden topsoil is a sandy loam containing a lot of organic matter. It is neither too sandy nor mostly clay, but somewhere in between. Ideally, apply the good topsoil 12-18 inches deep, but certainly no less than 6-8 inches to allow for strong, drought-resistant root growth. Grade the soil gently so it drains away from the foundation of your home.

If bringing in good topsoil is not an option, incorporate as much organic matter as possible into your existing soil. Organic matter includes decaying plant materials or manures that enrich and loosen soil, improve the drainage of clay soils, hold water and nutrients in sandy soils, slow down erosion, and provide a favorable environment for earthworms and beneficial microorganisms. As it decays, organic matter releases small amounts of nutrients back into the soil for plants to use. Peat moss, manure, and compost are some of the most common forms of organic material. Adding just a few inches of these products and working them in with a tiller can make a huge improvement in any poor, nutrient-deficient soil.

Soil Testing

Take your soil seriously. Poor infertile soil means poor non-productive plants. A healthy lawn is a result of fertile, healthy soil. Since turfgrass receives its primary nutrition from the soil, having your soil tested is a must. Otherwise you are "growing by guessing," and that can be costly financially, nutritionally, and environmentally. A soil test will measure the fertility of your soil and tell you what needs to be added.

Collect ten to fifteen samples of soil from a depth of 4-6 inches throughout your lawn area, then mix them together, and fill a pint jar with the mixture. Take the sample to your Cooperative Extension Service, which will send it to their state lab for analysis. Typically there is a small fee for the ser-

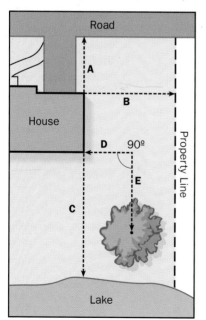

vice. In a few weeks, test results will be sent back with your soil's nutritional data along with adjustment recommendations and guidelines. Many of the soil nutrients and pH adjusters that may be needed are best worked into the soil prior to planting.

While waiting for the soil test results, calculate your total lawn area (minus any structures) in square feet, which is length multiplied by width. This is important information to use later in determining the amount of seed, sod, fertilizer, soil additives, or other materials needed to establish and care for your lawn.

Calculating Lawn Area

Lawns not only provide recreational space and accent landscape beds, they also control erosion, reduce glare and noise, absorb air pollution, and trap dust particles.

Cool or Hot, Shade or Not

Matching your grass selection to your growing zone and site is a key factor in developing a good lawn. There are two broad categories of turf that grow in the Southern United States—cool-season and warm-season grasses. The line between the areas where these two categories of grass do well is often called the transition zone. It falls along the northern boundaries of the southernmost states as seen on the Southern States Grass Zones map in the Introduction.

Cool-season turf is more cold hardy and grows best during the cooler fall, winter, and spring months of the year. These grasses typically remain green most of the winter but can occasionally brown or burn during extreme cold spells. Because they don't acclimate well to heat and drought, they can be grown somewhat successfully in partial shade.

Cool-season grasses usually grow in clumps that do not spread. Therefore, to keep a nice thick lawn, routine reseeding is needed, sometimes as often as once a year. This is best done either in the fall or spring. Fescue, Kentucky bluegrass, and ryegrass are cool-season grasses. They are usually successful in the Upper South, but they are not as commonly used in the Deep South because they cannot take the summer heat and drought. Supplemental irrigation, whether by hand or an automated sprinkler system, is a must to keep cool-season grasses from going dormant or dying completely in the heat of the summer.

Warm-season grasses, on the other hand, thrive in the South's summer heat. In the winter, they naturally go dormant, turning brown in the coldest of conditions. These grasses green up in the spring—sometimes late spring—as soil temperatures rise. All warm-season grasses can suffer some winter damage depending on how cold the temperatures become and how much soil moisture is available during the cold spell.

Bermudagrass, centipedegrass, St. Augustinegrass, and zoysiagrass are the most common warm-season grasses. Bahiagrass, buffalograss, and carpetgrass are also grown but not as widely. All these warm-season grasses spread by stolons (aboveground stems) and rhizomes (underground stems), eliminating the need for routine reseeding. Overall, warm-season grasses are more drought tolerant than cool-season grasses. They will also recuperate better if they should go dormant during extended dry periods.

Avoid combining permanent plantings of warm-season and cool-season grasses, such as bermudagrass and fescue. They have distinctly different growing periods, textures, mowing heights, and management requirements. Combining the two will just create twice the amount of work and will result in a patchy-looking lawn during most seasons of the year.

Observe shading patterns in your yard before selecting a grass. Most lawn grasses perform best with full sun all day. Partial or dappled shade (with shade four to six hours per day) limits the type of lawn you can plant. Don't even try a lawn grass in heavy shade (more than six hours a day) unless you are willing to do some tree work. Thinning trees or removing lower branches can increase the light and make grass a possibility even in fairly shady situations.

Prepare the Planting Site

Before planting grass, eliminate all undesirable weeds or grasses either mechanically or chemically. Mechanical techniques for removing weeds include digging, hoeing, and smothering. Covering the soil with black plastic for three to five months prior to planting prevents sunlight from reaching the ground, smothering existing weeds and grasses, while generating ample heat to kill weed seed. Tilling to remove existing vegetation will not work with plants that form underground stems, such as bermudagrass. The rhizomes and stolons scatter, then later root and grow. Tilling also brings more weed seeds to the surface where they will germinate.

Be aware of sunlight patterns in your yard. An area with dappled shade will limit the type of lawn you can grow there. Tall fescue and Kentucky bluegrass are the most shade tolerant of the turfgrasses.

Chemical approaches that include very specific herbicides are often the most complete eradication methods. Use a non-selective herbicide like glyphosate (the active ingredient in herbicides such as Roundup®) or glufosinate-ammonium (the active ingredient in the herbicide Finale®) according to label directions to kill any existing vegetation. Non-selective means the herbicide kills anything the spray reaches. But non-selective herbicides don't sterilize the soil, so you can replant once the existing vegetation is completely dead. Spraying herbicides should be done a few weeks, even months, before planting to allow the chemicals time to kill the entire plant, roots and all. Persistent weeds or grasses such as bermudagrass may require more than one spraying. Mixing an indicator dye (typically blue), available at turf or farm supply businesses, with the herbicide allows you to see where you have sprayed.

Remove large rocks, pebbles, or soil clods that may interfere with seed establishment. Large pieces of wood, tree branches, and bark should also be removed since they can contribute to a perplexing problem in lawns called "fairy ring," discussed in detail in Chapter Seven.

Once all vegetation is killed or removed, lightly work the top inch or so of soil just prior to planting by tilling very shallowly or raking by hand. Working the soil too deeply will stir up more weed seeds.

Other Considerations

If you live in a drought prone part of the South, which is pretty much all of the South, you should think about an irrigation system. A 5,000 square foot lawn can transpire about 3,000 gallons of water on a hot summer day, helping cool the area around it. But some of that water will need to be replaced or drought stress will occur, and the benefits of cooling will be lost.

Irrigation is an investment that can pay for itself in a couple of years in water and time saved.

How do you like your lawn grass—coarse or fine? Some folks just prefer the look and feel of fine-textured grasses such as bermudagrass or zoysiagrass to coarser types such as St. Augustine or fescue. And some grasses are assumed to be higher maintenance (zoysia, for example, although I have found that it doesn't necessarily need more mowing or fertilizing than other grasses). Categorizing lawn grasses according to maintenance is very subjective and depends on what you imagine a lawn should look like—sometimes it's a case of being more realistic in your expectations.

Seed, Sprig, Plug, or Sod

Most lawn grass varieties have several specific named cultivars from which to choose. The specific cultivar will dictate the method of planting depending on whether the grass is available as seed or strictly in vegetative form. Look for turfgrass with "certified" on the label for extra insurance that you are getting what you want. The planting bed should be prepared as described earlier whether you are seeding, sprigging, plugging, or laying sod. Specific seeding and vegetative planting rates are covered in Chapter Six.

Grasses available only in vegetative form either have no flowers or the flowers are typically sterile, so the grass must be reproduced by sprigs, plugs, or sod. Grasses available as seed are reproduced by pollination and seed collection.

When purchasing seed, read the label of the container to find the best purity ratings, which is a nice way of saying percentage of weed contamination. Generally, purchase grass seed with no more than 10 percent weed contamination. The germination rate of the grass seed should be around 85 percent.

After planting, make sure the seed comes in contact with the soil by lightly raking it to cover the seed at a depth of about $1/8$ inch. Firm the planting site, and provide even more soil-to-seed contact by tamping or rolling with a weighted roller. For more uniform coverage, apply half the seed in one direction and the remaining half at right angles to the first. Hand, drop, or rotary seeders are most commonly used, although drill seeders are also available. Small seed can be mixed with dry sand in about a 50/50 mix to make spreading easier.

Mulching with weed-free grain straw (oat, wheat, or barley) at a thickness of about $1-1^1/2$ inches is optional, but it does help retain soil moisture

Seed Application Pattern

and minimize erosion. Typically one bale of straw, weighing between 60-80 pounds, will cover about 1,000 square feet. Grain seed present in the straw may also germinate but usually dies out with mowing or increased summer temperatures. Do not use grass hay as mulch, or additional weed seed will be introduced. Hydro-seeding using machines that mix seed with water, and sometimes even mulch, is another option for establishing a lawn, especially on steeply sloping sites.

If you are planning a bermudagrass, zoysiagrass, or St. Augustinegrass lawn, you can find some cultivars in sprig form. Planting with sprigs is the least expensive of the vegetative planting methods. Sprigs are stems or runners with two or four nodes, or joints, and few to no roots. A node is the location on the stem where roots and shoots emerge. Rates and spacing vary depending on the type of grass, but sprigs are typically planted at a depth of about 1-2 inches. Sprigs are available commercially or can be harvested from existing turf or pulled from sod. One square yard or 9 square feet of sod can yield approximately one bushel of sprigs. This works out to be approximately 2,000 bermuda or zoysia sprigs and 500 St. Augustine or centipede sprigs. The sprigs can be furrowed into the soil, or they can be broadcast on the surface and top-dressed with a light covering of topsoil or organic material. Whichever method you use, the sprigs should have good soil contact. The ideal placement is to leave one-quarter of the sprig sticking out of the ground. The closer together the sprigs are placed, the faster they will cover the area.

Plugs are nothing more than small, cut pieces of sod usually 2-4 inches across, with a thickness of 2-3 inches of soil and roots. Unlike sprigs, plugs are seldom available commercially, but you can cut your own from either an existing lawn or a pallet of sod. In some regions of the country, grasses are available in flats, similar to flats of flowers, with individual containers of grass, also known as plugs. It takes three to ten times more material to plant a lawn with plugs than with sprigs. The following chart will help you determine the amount of sod to purchase if you are going to cut plugs. One square yard of sod yields approximately three hundred twenty-four 2-inch plugs.

Plugging can be done with both warm- and cool-season grasses, but is not recommended for cool-season, clumping grasses, such as fescue.. The plugs may be round or square depending on the plugging tool or machine. Plugs establish faster than sprigs because they are already well-rooted, but like sprigs, the more closely they are spaced, the quicker they will fill an area.

Plug Spacing	Number of Plugs/ 1,000 sq. ft.	Yards of Sod Required
6 inches	4,000	12+
8 inches	2,250	7
12 inches	1,000	3+

Sod is harvested turf, roots and all, cut into assorted sizes, then stacked or rolled on a pallet. Sod creates an instant lawn and is therefore more costly than any other method. But research shows that sod lawns are fifteen times more effective in controlling runoff than seeded lawns, even after three years. The planting bed should be prepared ahead of time even when laying sod. The roots establish faster in a prepared bed than on an unprepared site. Snugly fit

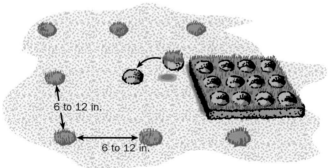

6 to 12 in.

6 to 12 in.

Grass Plug Placement

the sod pieces together in an alternating pattern so the seams do not line up. Avoid stretching the sod when you are laying it since it will shrink as it dries a bit and settles, causing voids in the lawn (although you should avoid letting the sod dry out). Most sod is sold by square yards per pallet with 50 yards per pallet being the norm. There are 9 square feet in a square yard of sod, so if you have 3,500 square feet of lawn to plant, you will need to order at least 388 yards of sod (3,500 ÷ 9 = 388). Roll or tamp the sod, (sprigs and plugs also) to ensure good soil contact, eliminating air pockets and leveling the soil. Roll at right angles to the direction the sod was laid.

Mixing sprigs with areas of plugs and sod can cause a slightly uneven lawn. Sprigged lawns seldom grow to the thickness of sod, so expect the surface to remain uneven, even years after planting. The unevenness can be detected when mowing or walking across the lawn surface.

Sod Placement

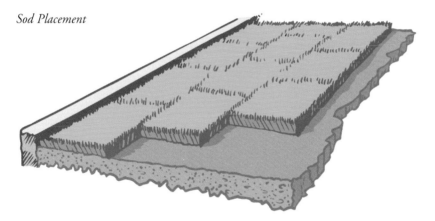

When to Plant Your Lawn

Seed, sprig, sod, or plug at the appropriate times of year. For warm-season grasses, that means the soil temperatures need to be approaching 70° F. A good guide is to plant when other warm-season grasses start to green up and grow. There must also be at least two months allowed for warm-season grasses to become established before winter. April through July is the ideal planting time for warm-season grasses assuming you have adequate rainfall or supply supplemental irrigation. Dormant sodding of warm-season grasses is sometimes done, but the chances for winter-kill are much greater since the roots have not penetrated the soil for extra protection.

Cool-season lawns can be planted in the very early spring between late February and early April or in the fall during September or October. Fall planting is preferred in order to give the grass a longer time to get established before the onset of the summer heat and drought. Cool-season lawns are usually started by seed although some varieties are available as sod. The sod squares are not as tight as the warm-season, rhizomatous grasses, so they are more likely to fall apart.

Post-Establishment Care

Gently water after planting, and keep the newly planted lawn moist but not soggy for at least ten to twenty-one days. Never allow seedlings, in particular, to dry out completely. This is best accomplished by daily light waterings. On windy, sunny days you may need to water two or three times per day depending on your soil type. Less irrigation will be needed if straw mulch is used. As the turf becomes more established, water deeply and less often.

Mow as soon as the grass, whether from seed, sprigs, plugs, or sod, reaches a height $^1/_3$ greater than the recommended mowing height for your particular variety. (Specific mowing guidelines are found in Chapter Six.) This will promote lateral spread and deep rooting. Do not mow when the grass is wet. Wet leaf blades are more likely to mat together or tear, and pull the plant, roots and all, out of the ground.

If you prepared your soil properly, any needed phosphorus, potassium, and lime were added prior to planting. These materials do not move readily through the soil and are best worked in at the root zone. If fertilizer was not applied before planting, a complete blend of nitrogen (N), phosphorus (P), and potassium (K) can be applied three to four weeks afterward. It will just take longer for the P, K, and lime to work. Any fertilizer mixture you use should be less than 10 percent nitrogen since a higher analysis can burn newly emerging seedlings.

On newly planted lawns it is best to pull or hoe any weeds. Frequent mowing, proper fertilization, and correct watering will also help. Any maintenance practices that help the grass cover the ground more quickly will also help shade out germinating weed seeds. Herbicides should be a last resort on a new lawn. If you decide to use one, read the label carefully since few are recommended for new lawns.

Renovating a Lawn

"Renovation" is the term for trying to get poorly performing lawns reestablished and back into shape. There are different levels of renovation. Partial renovation may be a simple process of seeding over thinning grass. Complete renovation is the most extreme form, and it basically means starting over from scratch. Some form of renovation is usually required when a lawn becomes thin and spotty or overgrown with undesirable weeds or grasses.

First find the cause of your lawn's problem. If the issue is pests, then properly identify them and treat the lawn accordingly. Pests are covered extensively in Chapter Seven. Many thinning, weed-infested lawns are the result of improper management or cultural practices. Take a soil test to determine if the problem is poor soil nutrition or improper pH. If the soil is compacted from heavy foot traffic or repetitious mowing patterns, then aerating the soil may be needed. This is covered in Chapter Four.

If correcting these problems does not help reestablish your existing grass, then replanting may be required. Choose the appropriate turfgrass cultivars for your site and growing conditions. Replanting can be done in localized areas or can encompass the entire lawn depending on the extent of the problem. In either case, use the same procedures described earlier to prepare a planting bed. Kill all the existing vegetation before replanting, especially if another invasive lawn species has encroached into the preferred lawn grass.

What Can Go Wrong When Planting a Lawn

Over-Watering	Over-Fertilization
Under-Watering	Under-Fertilization
Cold Temperatures	Compacted Soil
Hot Temperatures	Seed Blew or Washed Away
Seed Planted Too Deep or	Damping-off Disease
Too Shallow	Site Too Steep, Poor Water
Poor Soil Contact	Penetration
Improper Weed and Feed	Dog Spots
Applications	Birds
Use of Pre-emergent Herbicide	Insects

Watering

> **Know Your Soil Type**
>
> **Let Your Grass Tell You When to Water**
>
> **Water Deeply and Less Often**
>
> **Water Early**
>
> **Water Efficiently**
>
> **Condition Your Lawn for Drought**

Water-Holding Capacity of Soils

Loamy soils with a higher organic content have the best water-holding capacity. Sandy soils may hold too little water, while clay soils may hold too much. Knowing your soil type will help you manage your watering regimen better. If you weren't present during the soil preparation and planting period, use a soil probe or trowel to collect soil samples throughout the lawn and determine what type of soil you have. Keep in mind that the soil makeup of your lawn may vary from place to place, with pockets of sand, rock, or clay.

In most cases, simply touching and looking at the soil can determine its makeup. Does the soil run through your fingers, or compact into a ball when squeezed in your hand? Sandy soils tend to slip away, while clay soils compact. Digging a good-sized hole and filling it with water will also give you guidance as to the drainage properties of the soil. A hole that holds water for many hours indicates you have a heavy clay soil with poor drainage. A commercial soil-testing lab can also determine soil texture, or you can do a simple home test and get pretty close.

Simple Home Test to Determine Soil Makeup

Your soil texture, along with other factors, affects the frequency and amount of water needed to maintain your lawn. The texture of a soil is determined by the proportions of the three main mineral components—sand, silt, and clay. Loamy soils are a mix of the three, ideal for most plants, including turf. A simple test to determine your soil texture is based on the weight of these particles when settled out of a water suspension. Sand is heavier than silt, and silt is heavier than clay, due to particle size. They will settle at various levels and times because of their differences in weight. This enables you to gauge the percentage of each in a soil sample.

Fill a quart jar 2/3 full of water, and add one teaspoon of wetting agent or surfactant to separate or disperse the soil particles. Liquid dishwashing detergent will work as a surfactant.

Add soil until the jar is nearly full. Leave some air space to allow for shaking. Remove any debris such as rocks, roots, or gravel. Break up any clods to help speed up the process. Shake the jar vigorously, or stir the mixture with a spoon to make sure the soil and water are mixed thoroughly.

When the water and soil are completely mixed, vigorously shake the jar for a couple of minutes, and set it on a level surface. After about forty seconds the sand will settle. Mark the sand level with a permanent or waterproof marker on the outside of the jar. The time to mark the jar is when the settled sand particles are not moving, but the silt and clay are still in suspension, which can be hard to distinguish.

Wait another four hours without disturbing the jar, and most of the silt will be settled. Mark the silt level with the pen. The remainder that settles in the next twenty-four hours should be clay. Mark again to identify the clay level.

Observe the thickness of the three distinct sections. In general, if all three layers are about equal your soil is loamy, if the top layer is the deepest your soil is mostly clay, and if the bottom layer is the deepest your soil is sandy.

DROUGHT TOLERANCE of Southern Turfgrasses

Bermudagrass	*excellent*
Carpetgrass	*fair*
Centipedegrass	*fair*
St. Augustinegrass	*fair*
Zoysiagrass	*fair*
Kentucky Bluegrass	*fair*
Tall Fescue	*poor*

Looking at your jar of soil, assign a percentage to each layer with the percentages totaling one hundred. Use the following Soil Texture Triangle graph to determine the overall texture or makeup of your soil.

Soil Texture Triangle

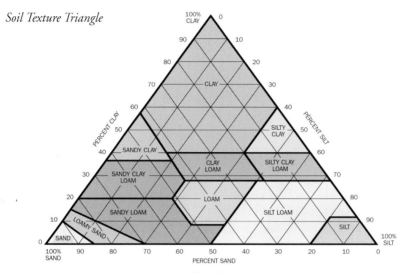

Source: Soil Science Society of America

The dark black lines identify the twelve most common soil textures. Follow the angle of the directional lines shown on the outside of the graph when keying in your percentages of sand, silt, and clay. The soil texture category where they intersect is the primary makeup of your soil.

As an example, suppose your jar of soil came to 20 percent sand, 70 percent silt, and 10 percent clay. At the bottom of the diagram, which is sand, you would follow the line for 20 up and to the left. On the right, or silt, side, mark 70 and follow the line down. The remaining 10 would be located on the left, or clay, side, so follow the line straight across to the right. In this example the three lines come together under "silt loam." So the soil makeup is primarily silt loam, which has fairly good water holding capacity.

It's Time to Water

Let your lawn tell you when to water. No, not verbally (although that would be nice) but by sight. Grass plants are 75-80 percent water, (grass clippings are almost 90 percent water by weight). As a result, the plants show obvious signs of stress that are very useful in determining when it's time to water.

Especially with coarser varieties, the grass leaf blades fold in half vertically when they need water. The grass foliage also will start to turn a dull gray color. Lastly, observe your footprints after you walk across the lawn. If the grass immediately pops back up, there is enough moisture in the leaf blades to sustain the plants a little longer. The grass needs water if the footprints remain compressed for a while. Water when you see one or more of these signs, but not before. Providing lawns with too much water actually makes it harder for them to take the summer heat and drought, not to mention wasting water and money.

Your soil texture, grass type, management style, rainfall, air and soil temperatures, wind, and humidity can all affect the amount and frequency of watering you will need to do.

How Much Water?

Watering deeply for long periods of time and less frequently is best for your lawn. Light, frequent watering produces shallow, weak root systems. Apply enough water at one time to soak the soil to a depth of at least 6-8 inches, which is equivalent to 1-1^1/$_2$ inches of water per week. This may need to be increased at the peak of summer, depending on the soil type, sun, heat intensity, and slope of the yard. (Remember also to take into account water restrictions in your area.) For many sprinklers, this means letting them run for two or three hours. At the same time, be careful to not water too much. Over-watering can leach plant nutrients, especially nitrogen, past the root zone, and in extreme cases can cause a lack of oxygen and limit root growth.

The best way to know how much water your irrigation system is putting out is to measure it. Place numerous shallow containers such as tuna cans or pie plates randomly around the watering range of your irrigation system. Leave the system on for thirty minutes. Then measure the water in each container using a ruler, and figure the average depth in all the containers combined. If the system puts out an average of $1/2$ inch of water in thirty minutes, you know you need to leave it on for an hour to get an inch of water, or two hours for 2 inches.

If all else fails, use a soil probe or trowel to sample 6 inches into the soil, and look to see how far down the water is penetrating in the allotted test time. Then adjust your watering accordingly.

If sloped, compacted, or heavy soil causes the water to run off before it can penetrate, either move the sprinkler to another site and come back later, or set your timed sprinkler to water for a couple of different periods for shorter lengths of time. Never water a lawn every day unless you are establishing or renovating it.

Measuring Irrigation
Water Output

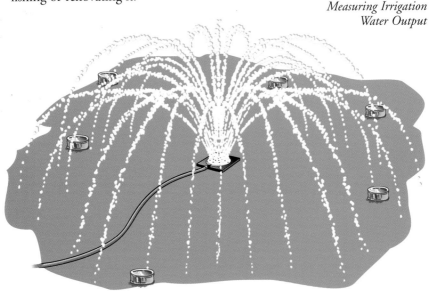

When to Water

Without a doubt, the best time to water is before sunrise, between 2:00 and 8:00 in the morning. This is why an automatic timer comes in handy; otherwise you will need to be up before the crack of dawn. Of course, the exact time to start supplemental irrigation using an automated system will be dictated by the number of watering zones and length of time each zone is set to run, or, if you are using the hand method, by how early you can get out of bed.

Studies show water loss during early morning irrigation is 50 percent less than during the day or evening. There is also less risk of disease. Irrigating after dew forms on turf typically does not increase the chances of disease. But irrigating before dew forms, such as in the evening when you get home from work, prolongs the length of time the grass blades are wet, thus increasing the chances of disease problems. Watering grass in the heat of the day increases the risk of drift and evaporation but does not burn foliage as many people believe.

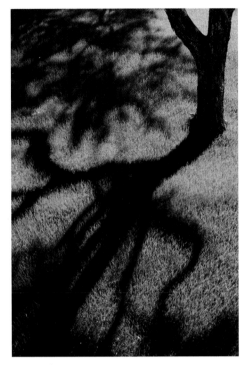

Early morning is the best time to water your lawn.

If a lawn is severely compacted, water penetration will be limited. Aerating the lawn is a good way to correct soil compaction, but it should be done when the grass is actively growing early in the season rather than during periods of drought or high heat. Guidelines on aeration are covered in Chapter Four.

Invest in an Irrigation System

Water-efficient irrigation designs and sprinkler heads are becoming more common. Rely on a professional, and get several estimates if you are not a do-it-yourself kind of gardener. However, there are plenty of good references and product guides to help you design and install your own irrigation system. Just remember that with lawns, especially, it is tempting to put in a few of the pulsating heads, or ones with higher flow rates that cover a wide area. Systems that spray fine droplets of water across long distances are not, however, the most efficient. Sprinklers that emit large drops of water closer to the ground are best. It may require more sprinklers per site, but the money saved in water usage and by the plants using the water more efficiently will easily cover the cost of the system in the long run. To help your pocketbook, put in a few zones at a time, leaving connections for future expansion. Avoid poor designs that water the hardscape such as driveways, sidewalks, and buildings. Learn to adjust and reset your timers, since new lawns are watered differently than established ones. Consider incorporating a rain sensor device to avoid watering in the rain.

Investing in an automated irrigation system can pay for itself in a few years.

Preparing Your Lawn for Drought

The easiest way to deal with drought is to select a grass that is drought tolerant. Simple things like proper watering, raising the mowing height during drought and heat stress, mowing more frequently, and reducing or eliminating fertilizer and herbicides will also help.

The key to helping your grass survive or tolerate severe drought is to condition it so it doesn't need pampering. Remember that watering deeply and less often encourages deeper roots that are more drought tolerant. Gradually raising the mowing height 25 to 50 percent will also encourage deeper roots and help shade the soil. And by all means keep the lawn mower blades sharp. Torn leaf blades cause even more moisture loss and stress to the plants.

Fertilizer is not a cure-all, either. Within reason, it is good for the roots and stimulates new growth, but during drought periods and high soil and air temperatures it can have detrimental effects. A fertilizer analysis that is more than 10 percent nitrogen can burn both foliage and roots during drought. At the same time, it can stimulate growth that is not as conditioned to or tolerant of heat stress. Nitrogen fertilizers should never be applied to cool-season grasses during hot summer weather, since the grass is already under stress from the heat.

Attempting to maintain your entire lawn during times of severe water shortage is not always practical. If water rationing should occur, determine the priority areas in your lawn. You may want to water the portion that receives the most traffic or is used for summer recreation. The lawn closest to the house may also be a priority to help filter dust or to serve as a fire retardant.

Of course going dormant from drought is the natural way grass avoids stress. But during this dormancy your grass will not be green, sun-germinating weed seed can prevail, and with severe stress the plants can even die.

Ways to Save Water

Reduce Slopes or Berms in the Lawn

Avoid Runoff Situations

Test and Amend Soil

Add Organic Material as Topdressing Whenever Possible

Install a Water-Efficient Irrigation System

Select Drought-Tolerant Grass

Sod Rather Than Seed

Water Early in the Morning

Minimize Fertilizer

Mow High

Fertilizing

> **Apply Only What Is Needed**
>
> **Choose a Maintenance Level**
>
> **Apply at Appropriate Time of Year**
>
> **Don't Apply When Leaves Are Wet**
>
> **Don't Apply When Grass Is Stressed**
>
> **Split Rates in Half and Apply in Two Different Directions**
>
> **Water Summer Applications Thoroughly**
>
> **Be Careful with Weed-and-Feed Combinations**
>
> **Consider Organic or Slow-Release Products**

The more you feed, the more you MOW! Fertilize the lawn every four to six weeks to keep it green? Just how green does a lawn need to be? Mine is green, and I feed it once a year. Sure, it is true that grass plants need nitrogen but within reason. Base your fertilizing practices on 1) soil test results, 2) soil texture, 3) grass variety, 4) cost of fertilizer per pound, 5) rate of release, 6) ease of application, 7) safety to plants and environment, and 8) how much you like to mow.

There are three levels of fertility maintenance that should be considered for a lawn care program. Some lawn care companies suggest even more. These levels should coincide with soil test results and your particular growing region. The levels and months to apply shown in Table 3.1 in the appendix are only guidelines. Let your lawn grass be the major factor in deciding when to apply. Wait until the grass has completely greened up and you are past the last frost date.

The high maintenance program, also known as the full fertilization treatment, typically includes three to four feedings per year. The medium or moderate level includes two feedings, and the low or light program involves only one. I often hear the light program referred to as "the lazy gardener's method." I typically practice the low maintenance program myself, and I'm anything but lazy. I prefer to call it "the common sense method."

The last time I tried the high maintenance program with four fertilizations in one year, I had to sleep with a knife next to my bed for about a month out of fear that the grass was going to come in and get me! But if you like to mow the lawn a couple of times a week, frequent feedings will help you do just that.

Sweet or Sour

Plant growth is affected by the degree of alkalinity (sweetness) or acidity (sourness) of the soil. Soil pH is the mechanism used to measure how alkaline or acidic the soil is. The pH scale ranges from 1–14 with 7 being neutral. Anything below 7 is acidic, and anything above is alkaline or basic. The scale is also logarithmic, meaning the distance from one number to the next is compounded. For example, a pH of 5 is 10 times more acidic than a pH of 6 and 100 times more acidic than a pH of 7.

Plant sensitivity to soil pH depends on many factors, including the type of plant, soil type, and environmental conditions. A soil test to determine the existing pH is crucial so you can make the adjustments needed to allow plants to maximize existing soil nutrients and any future fertilizer applications. If the

Changing Soil pH

Lowering the pH of Sandy Loam Soils to 5.5		Raising the pH of Sandy Loam Soils to 6.5	
Existing Soil pH*	Pounds of Soil Sulfur per 100 Square Feet**	Existing Soil pH***	Pounds of Lime per 100 Square Feet
9.0	7.5	6.0	2.0
8.5	6.0	5.5	4.0
8.0	5.5	5.0	6.0
7.5	5.0	4.5	8.0
7.0	3.5		
6.5	1.5		

*Based on an initial soil test. Some variation will be needed depending on soil type. Clay soils require heavier applications. Never apply more than five pounds of sulfur at one time if plants are present. Wait several weeks to apply the remainder. Total amounts can be applied to new, vacant planting sites.

**Approximate, buffered pH will dictate amount of material needed.

***Based on an initial soil test. Silt loam and clay loam soils will require heavier applications. Dolomitic, Ag, or pelletized lime products are easier to apply. Avoid hydrated lime for safety reasons.

soil pH is not in the particular plant's preferred range, it can interfere with the plant's ability to absorb nutrients. Extreme pH ranges beyond a plant's tolerance level can also weaken the plant, making it more susceptible to disease, insect attack, and environmental stresses.

The pH of a soil is typically raised by applying liming materials and lowered by applying sulfur products and certain fertilizers. The amount should be based on a soil test that identifies the current soil pH (based on buffered pH results). The soil type and the amount of organic matter it contains also influence the quantity of amendments needed. The process of changing soil pH typically takes months if you are starting a new lawn or renovating an existing one.

Essential Nutrients

There are sixteen nutrients or elements essential for proper plant growth. In turf care, we focus primarily on the major three of nitrogen (N), phosphorus (P), and potassium (K), although the minor or secondary nutrients of calcium, magnesium, sulfur, iron, manganese, boron, molybdenum, copper, zinc, and chlorine are also important. Carbon, hydrogen, and oxygen are non-mineral nutrients derived primarily from air and water.

Nitrogen produces healthy leaf and root growth, stimulates leaf color and density, and assists in resilience to other stresses. Of course, the application timing and amount are important. Excessive nitrogen can encourage rapid leaf growth at the expense of root growth. It can also contribute to disease and insect infestation, thatch accumulation, and reduced heat and cold tolerance.

Phosphorus plays a critical role in establishing the root systems of lawn grasses. It is also helpful in energy transformation within the plant. Like nitrogen, excessive amounts of phosphorus can cause problems. Potassium is also associated with the health of the plant's root system and it is thought to play an even more vital role in the plant's ability to withstand environmental and mechanical stress.

What to Feed

Once again, a soil test will help determine the needs of your soil, which in turn nourishes your lawn grass. Try to match the fertilizer product available from your farm supply or garden center to the guidelines your soil test recommends.

Fertilize grass when it is actively growing. For warm-season grasses that means fertilizing between March and October, for cool-season grasses, between September and May.

Oftentimes, test results indicate that only nitrogen is needed. If nitrogen is needed, evaluate your expectations for the growth of your lawn and the amount of work you want to devote to its care. Then match those conditions with the particular fertilizer maintenance program that best suits your time and money and the current health of your lawn. Keep in mind that nitrogen is a highly transitional nutrient in the soil and is hard to measure in a lab.

Test results can also indicate that phosphorus and potassium are needed. These products are relatively slow to move through the soil and take time to improve the health of your lawn. Routine applications of a fertilizer high in P or K, such as 10-20-10, when they are not needed can be detrimental to your grass and the environment, not to mention being a waste of money and time.

Any product over-applied haphazardly with the excess left on sidewalks and driveways likely will wash into storm drains and potential water supplies. Fertilize sensibly, and let a soil test guide you as to how much is needed rather than just guessing.

When to Feed

The grass is pretty good at telling you when to fertilize, just as it can tell you when it is time to water. Chlorotic yellow or dull green blades combined with non-vigorous growth is a good indication that a fertilizer application would be beneficial. But look at the whole picture. Stress due to compacted soil needs to be corrected, or a fertilizer application will not do much good. The grass cannot utilize the nutrients effectively if other factors are contributing to its symptoms.

Rainfall and temperature also dictate when to fertilize. Drought-plagued lawns fed in the heat of the summer risk being burned or even more stressed unless regular supplemental irrigation can be provided. But be sure to water the lawn after and not before feeding. Fertilizer tends to stick to wet leaves. Applying fertilizer when leaf blades are wet can burn or speckle the foliage, impacting the overall appearance of your lawn.

Warm-season lawns typically are actively growing between March and October, depending on your location. Any fertilizer applications should be made during this time period. Experts discourage feeding bermuda lawns late in the season if they are prone to spring dead spot. Heavy and late applications of fertilizer high in nitrogen stimulate growth that is more susceptible to the fungal organism that causes dead spot. More details on this and other diseases are in Chapter Seven.

Cool-season grasses tend to grow best between September and May, so schedule feedings during these times except during the coldest months. Fertilizing outside the recommended months can stimulate unwanted weed growth and reduce grass hardiness.

Water your lawn after you have applied fertilizer, but not before. Applying fertilizer on wet grass can burn the foliage.

Weed and Feed

I'm not a big fan of weed-and-feed products for the South. They are convenient, but they also entice homeowners to fertilize warm-season grasses earlier than needed. Many people tout weed-and-feed applications early in the spring before the warm-season grasses really start to green up and grow. Depending on what weeds you are trying to control, you may also buy a product that is for crabgrass prevention and not the unsightly spring weeds already growing. As a result, you end up feeding the winter weeds instead of eliminating them.

Weed-and-feed products control different weeds depending on their active ingredient. Some control existing cool-season winter weeds as a post-emergent, after they are already up and growing. Others prevent warm-season annual weeds, including broadleaf weeds, from germinating by acting as a pre-emergent. You definitely must know which weeds you are trying to control or prevent, and select a product accordingly.

Organic Versus Manmade

Contrary to popular belief, plants do not know the difference between organic fertilizers and man-made, synthetic fertilizers. Both are broken down by soil organisms into water-soluble materials available to the plants. Nonetheless, I lean toward organic products because of their slow-release action and benefits to the soil.

Slow release means the nitrogen is not available to the plant quickly. Rather, it must be broken down over time by soil microbes, moisture, and the proper temperatures. Quick-release fertilizers easily dissolve in water and are immediately available for plant use as long as too much water doesn't push the nitrogen down past the root zone.

Ammonium nitrate, 33-0-0, is an example of a synthetic, laboratory-produced nitrogen fertilizer. Such synthetic, inorganic nitrogen carriers have both pros and cons. Advantages include quick availability to the plant and thus a quick plant response. In other words, the plants green up faster. This is especially important in the case of nitrogen-deficiency stress and symptoms such as yellow, chlorotic color combined with stunted growth. Typically, synthetic water-soluble fertilizers don't depend on temperature to work, and they are reasonably priced.

Disadvantages include greater likelihood of loss from leaching caused by excess water, lowering of soil pH by fertilizers with ammonia, high foliar burn potential, and a rapid surge in plant growth, requiring more mowing. Such products can be used more effectively by applying smaller amounts more often, instead of applying the entire recommended amount at once.

Natural organic fertilizers include decayed living materials, sewage sludge, manure, and bone meal (see TABLE 3.2 in the appendix). The breakdown of these nutrients in the soil depends heavily on soil microorganisms. Natural organic fertilizers produce less foliar burn, very little leaching, and longer-lasting, more even growth of the grass. On the other hand, they are typically low in analysis and require larger amounts of product application. They are also slower to impact a plant if a deficiency is present, and they do not break down as effectively in cooler temperatures. Other, even unpleasant, results can be objectionable odors and the possible presence of salts, heavy metals, and weed seeds.

Other slow-release products, in addition to natural organics, include methylene urea, urea formaldehyde, sulfur-coated urea (SCU), polymer coated urea (PCU), and isobutylidine diurea (IBDU).

Winterizing Your Lawn

Some experts believe that fall fertilization is a creative way for garden centers to generate business at an otherwise slow time of year. However, it is thought that phosphorus (P) and potassium (K) can help promote a healthy root system, which in turn enables the grass to tolerate cold better. But keep in mind that it takes time for P and K to become available for the plant to use, so fall applications may not benefit the grass until later in the winter or even spring depending on the formulation. Applying P and K that are not needed can harm the environment and certainly wastes time and money. My recommendation is to rely on your soil test. If phosphorus and potassium are needed, then a fall application would be fine unless you did one in the spring or the previous fall. And if you routinely apply a complete fertilizer each spring, skip the fall application altogether. Be especially careful in applying fertilizer that is over 20 percent nitrogen in the fall. This can stimulate growth that is more susceptible to winter injury. Most winterizing formulations are 7-14 percent nitrogen. Personally I try to keep the fertilizer analysis at 10 percent nitrogen or less if a fall application is needed. Also remember that problems with spring dead spot on bermuda lawns are connected to late fall applications of fertilizer.

Reading a Fertilizer Bag

Fertilizers are sold based on the three main nutrients. The first number on the bag is nitrogen, the second number is phosphorus, and the third is potassium. For example, a bag of 10-20-10 would have 10 percent of the total weight as nitrogen (NO_3 or NH_4), 20 percent phosphorus (P_2O_5), and 10 percent potassium (K_2O). The remaining weight to reach 100 percent could be secondary nutrients like iron, sulfur, and magnesium, and filler materials to bind the nutrients into a form that is easy to apply. A fertilizer containing all three nutrients is referred to as a "complete" fertilizer. Fertilizers with any nutrient missing, such as 45-0-0 or 13-0-44, are considered incomplete fertilizers.

Fertilizer analyses are also referred to by the ratio of nutrients. For example, 10-20-10 would have a ratio of 1:2:1, 16-4-8 would be 4:1:2, and 17-17-17 would have a 1:1:1 ratio. If your soil test results suggest a fertilizer with a 3:1:2 ratio, you know you will need a fertilizer similar to 12-4-8.

Each fertilizer bag must have a label clearly stating the ingredients of the contents. This statement shows the amount of each nutrient and its form. Slow-release, controlled-release, or water-insoluble forms of nitrogen are identified on the label, which also shows the percentage of the nutrient that is in slow-release form. Comparing the amounts of slow-release nitrogen to the price per pound of the fertilizer can help you make better buying decisions. Expect slow-release products to be higher in cost but well worth the investment.

How Much to Apply

Fertilizer application rates are based on 1 pound of actual nitrogen per 1,000 square feet. For example, if you were using a complete fertilizer with an analysis of 13-13-13, the application rate would be 7.7 pounds of fertilizer per 1000 square feet, since it contains only 13 percent actual nitrogen, not 100 percent. This was calculated by dividing 1 by 0.13, or dividing 100 by 13. This formula works no matter what the nitrogen, phosphorus, or potassium amount.

Another way to determine the amount to use and buy for your particular lawn is shown below.

1 divided by amount of actual nitrogen in fertilizer bag (% ÷ 100)	÷	standard rate of 1000	×	sq. ft. of your lawn	=	amount to buy

So if the analysis is 13-13-13 and you have a 2,000 square foot lawn, the formula would be:

1 divided by 0.13 (13 ÷ 100) is 7.69	÷	1000	×	2,000 sq. ft.	=	15.38 pounds

Many brands of fertilizer show application rates on the bag that fall into the high maintenance category or are greater than needed at any one time. So figuring the rate ahead of time based on the actual percent of nitrogen available in your particular fertilizer bag is always a good idea (see TABLE 3.3 in the appendix).

Split the application amount over the entire growing season if you use organic fertilizers with very low nitrogen so that large quantities are not needed for your lawn at any one application.

How to Apply

With granular fertilizer, apply half the amount in one direction and the other half in the opposite direction to minimize skips and burns, similar to the seeding techniques discussed in Chapter One. There still may be some overlap and a few skips, but this is better than applying the fertilizer too heavily in one direction and causing dark green stripes in the lawn.

There are more scientific ways to apply fertilizer uniformly, but I have found that with smaller lawns, a hand-held broadcast applicator or seeder works nicely. I weigh the applicator empty and then weigh it again after it is filled with the granular product, so I know how much I am applying based on my prefigured rate. For larger lawns, drop and rotary spreaders are the norm.

Different levels of fertilizer maintenance will achieve different results, and require varying amounts of work. Choose a program that suits your lifestyle and expectations.

Liquid fertilizer applied through hose-end applicators is also available and should be used in accordance with label directions. It is possible to over-apply and burn the grass even with liquids. Liquid fertilizer N-P-K selections are very similar and may not match soil test recommendations, while granular types have a broader range of nutrient percentages to choose from and allow you to match soil deficiencies more closely. Applying phosphorus and potassium in liquid form when they are not needed is a waste of money and may have adverse effects on the lawn and even on the environment.

Calibrating Fertilizer Spreaders

Brand-name spreaders will have instructions or settings for applying different rates of fertilizers. Some fertilizer bags even tell you the settings to use for particular kinds of spreaders. These settings should be checked periodically for accuracy.

The easiest way to calibrate a spreader is to fill the hopper with a pre-weighed amount of fertilizer to a noted level and apply that amount over a pre-measured 1,000 square foot area (20 ft. × 50 ft.). Weigh the amount left in the hopper, and subtract it from the initial amount. The initial amount weighed minus the amount left equals the amount applied per 1,000 square feet. Notice the setting or dial on the spreader to see if it agrees with your calculations. If your spreader uses 5 pounds per thousand square feet, then you have a guide for future applications. You may need to adjust the control for the actual application to get the recommended amount. The calibration test also can be done using a 500 square foot space. Just multiply the amount used by two to convert it to 1,000 square feet. The type of spreader and how fast you walk will have some bearing on the consistency of the amount applied. Drop spreaders cover smaller areas but are more uniform in application. Rotary spreaders cover more area but tend to throw the fertilizer more to one side.

You can also calibrate by applying fertilizer on a 20 × 50 (1,000 square foot) or 10 × 50 (500 square foot) plastic tarp. Any dimensions equaling 500 or 1,000 square feet will work. The fertilizer can then be collected and weighed. You also will be able to see the throwing patterns of your particular spreader.

Many fertilizers and pH adjustment products are very dusty. Wearing gloves, a dust mask, and eye protection while applying them is strongly advised whether the product is synthetic or natural.

Mowing

Chapter Four

> **Mow Often**
>
> **Mow High**
>
> **Use a Sharp Blade**
>
> **Mow in Alternating Directions**
>
> **Recycle Clippings**
>
> **Invest in an Earth-Friendly Mower**
>
> **Consider a Mulching Mower or Blade**
>
> **Push, Don't Ride**

Hi-ho, hi-ho, it's off to work I go...and then I come home and mow the lawn! Mowing is the single most stressful practice for the grass—and the owner—in lawn care. Yet it is done more frequently than any other practice, generally taken for granted, and more often than not done incorrectly.

Mow Often

Most homeowners mow every seven to ten days. But if the truth be told, we really should be mowing every four to five days, especially if you follow the "one-third" rule, which says to mow when the lawn gets $1/3$ taller than the recommended growing height. For example, if you want to maintain your lawn at 2 inches, you should mow when the leaf blades reach 3 inches, so you are removing only $1/3$ of the blade at each mowing. That is all well and good, but unfortunately for those of us who mow every Saturday, no one told our grass to grow only $1/3$ above its optimum height between mowings. For my lawn, using the $1/3$ rule would mean mowing every four days during the growing season, even with minimal fertilization. But I do find that more frequent mowings keep the lawn in the best shape. The smaller clippings easily fall into the grass, quickly breaking down with sunlight and moisture. Realistically, it is tough for even professional lawn companies to mow that often, but if you get as close as possible to following the $1/3$ rule, success will be just around the corner.

Mow Then Measure

It is a good idea to measure the actual leaf blade length following mowing to determine exactly how the height compares to the mower deck setting you are using. Most mowers have mechanisms that allow adjustments to raise or lower the body of the mower. Instead of just depending on guesswork to find the right setting, take a ruler and measure the height of the grass blades in several locations immediately after mowing. The ground level will vary across your lawn, so an average measurement will give you a better idea of the height at which each setting really cuts.

Measuring the mower on a sidewalk or driveway will give an incorrect reading. You'll be cutting closer than this measurement indicates since the wheels of the mower sit down in the grass when you mow.

Mow High

One common mistaken belief is that the closer you cut the lawn, the slower it will grow, so you won't have to mow as often. If you keep cutting the grass so short you are almost scalping it, you may not have to mow as often, because it will likely die. The effect of mowing too close is that weeds will take over, and you will have to mow even more frequently. The more sunlight that reaches the soil surface, the more weed seed that germinates. Taller grass also filters pollutants better and serves as a living mulch for the lawn, minimizing soil temperatures and reflective heat.

Mowing grass high encourages deeper root systems, which are better able to withstand environmental stresses.

A sudden reduction in mowing height can be traumatic to your lawn. Changing the balance between top growth and roots shocks the plants, thus weakening their overall health and growth. If the grass becomes too tall, gradually reduce the cutting height over several mowings until the recommended height is reached.

Generally, grass roots mirror the grass blades, so the taller the blades, the deeper the roots. You want the roots to be deep because that will make the grass more drought, cold, and pest resistant. Follow recommended mowing heights in Chapter Six, preferably using the higher numbers. When trying to grow grass in shade, mow higher than recommended, and do the same when grass is stressed from drought and heat. And it is even a good idea to raise the mowing height gradually as fall arrives to give the turf more protection for winter.

Sharp Blades Are Better

Have you changed your lawn mower blades lately? Dull blades chew, rip, or tear grass blades. So if you haven't sharpened or replaced your blades and think you are mowing at a particular height, you are fooling yourself. Torn blades of grass often die back to below the tear, making the blade shorter than the original cut. Shredded grass blades are also more likely to succumb to disease problems, and they are more susceptible to heat and drought stress because they lose more water through transpiration. Sharp mower blades also save on fuel consumption. According to one study, mowing with sharp blades can reduce fuel use by as much as 20 percent.

Sharp mower blades give a clean, smooth cut. They also make the mowing process more efficient, causing less stress both on the mower and the grass. The easiest way to keep blades sharp is to buy an extra set and switch blades every few times you mow. Also start with new blades each year. This is a minimal investment that pays big dividends in the health of your lawn.

When changing mower blades, disconnect the spark-plug wire. A "c" clamp available at any hardware store can keep the blades from turning while you are loosening and tightening the bolts. There is even a Blade Buster™ tool made especially for this purpose. The worst thing to do is try holding the blades, dull or not, with your hands, even wearing gloves. These tools or something similar can help prevent serious cuts to your hands and fingers.

Rotary vs. Reel Mowers

Rotary	Reel
Initial low cost	*Low yearly cost (no gas or oil)*
Easy to maneuver	*Good for grasses needing lower cuts*
Basic maintenance	*Only maintenance is sharpening blades*
Ideal for uneven surfaces	*Smooth cut (better on level ground)*
No raking (with mulching mowers)	*No emissions*

Don't Be Set in Your Ways

Soil compaction occurs over time, usually from the weight of mowing or gardening equipment, pet runs, or frequent foot traffic. Areas near sidewalks and pathways are likely to become compacted first. Soil type also plays a role. Clay soils are more likely to compact than sandy, silty, or loamy soils. Soil com-

Vary your mowing patterns in order to prevent soil compaction. If you mow in one direction one week, then mow perpendicular or diagonal to that the next week.

paction causes problems such as poor root growth, poor oxygen penetration to the roots, and poor water filtration, all of which mean poor plant performance.

One of the biggest contributors to soil compaction in your lawn is mowing in the same direction week after week, year after year. It is easy to change directions every time you mow. If you first mow in a perpendicular direction, then the next time in a diagonal one, you can go at least four different ways, spreading the path of the lawnmower tires over a larger surface area. You'll also be surprised at how different the view looks when you vary the direction of your mowing.

To Bag or Not to Bag?

A 1,000 square foot lawn can generate 200 pounds or more of clippings annually depending on how often you fertilize. The clippings contain nutrients somewhere around 4 percent nitrogen (N), 2 percent potassium (P), and 0.5 percent phosphorus (K). So it doesn't make much sense to pay to fertilize the lawn, then cut the grass, and throw away part of the fertilizer. Frequent mowing, minimal feedings, and proper watering practices allow you to leave the clippings where they fall and benefit the lawn at the same time. If you shred the clippings with a mulching mower, you can reduce your fertilizer needs by as much as 25 percent.

On the other hand, leaving thick clumps of grass on the lawn after mowing can be detrimental, causing the grass underneath to yellow, brown, and possibly die. This practice also encourages disease and mold and can contribute to superficial root, rhizome, and stolon formation, resulting in thatch problems, especially if large quantities are left on a regular basis. If rain, vacation, or other causes permit your grass to get too tall between mowings, you most likely will need to rake and remove the clippings unless you use a mulching mower.

Mulching mowers and mulching blades pulverize and shred cut grass into smaller pieces, which helps eliminate the need for bagging or removing lawn clippings. Mulching mowers take less time than bagging, since you don't have to stop to empty a bag every few rounds. But bagging certainly is easier than raking and removing by hand. Mulching mowers must be pushed or driven more slowly than other mowers to allow time for the clippings to be chopped up properly. Immediately mowing the lawn a second time at a higher deck setting can also help disperse clippings so they will decay quickly. Of course, the effectiveness of all these methods depends on the amount of accumulated clippings.

Many municipalities limit or even prohibit grass clippings from their landfills in order to encourage recycling or composting of this valuable organic garden product. Use caution when applying clippings from a lawn recently treated with a post-emergent herbicide as a mulch for vegetables and flowers. It is better to compost these clippings thoroughly before use, turning the pile often to encourage heat and microorganisms to break down the chemicals.

Thatch—The Real Story

Thatch consists of layers of undecayed grass located between the soil and the leaf blades of the turf plants. Thatch is primarily composed of roots, rhizomes, and stolons, not grass clippings. Thatch formation is a routine part of the growth cycle, in which plant parts age, die, and decompose into humus. The problem occurs when something upsets this natural cycle, causing thatch to build up quicker than it can break down. Rapid, excessive lawn growth is the major cause of thatch, and over-fertilization and over-watering are the biggest culprits. They produce excessive amounts of grass clippings, preventing normal breakdown of thatch.

Excessive thatch inhibits water penetration into the soil, harbors insects and diseases, and leads to shallow root systems susceptible to heat, cold, and drought. The potential for thatch to become a problem depends on the turf-grass species and managment practices. A $1/2$ inch layer of thatch might be a

Grass with Thatch Layer

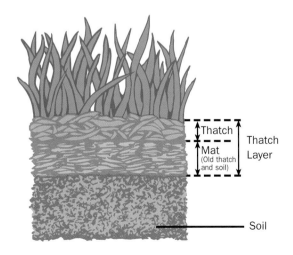

Thatch

Mat
(Old thatch and soil)

Thatch Layer

Soil

problem for some grasses, but not others. To determine the thickness, take plugs from your lawn so you can easily see and measure the thatch layer.

If you have too much thatch, there are several ways to deal with it. Vertical mowers and dethatching equipment, which can be rented from tool centers or home centers, mechanically reduce the thatch layer. They have blades, knives, or tines that lift the dead vegetation to the surface where it can be gathered, then composted. You can also use a hand-rake to pull thatch to the surface, but it is very time consuming, strenuous work, and most people don't do it vigorously enough to deal with severe thatch buildup. Some people scalp the grass in spring to loosen thatch, but since this can also encourage weed seed to germinate, it isn't a recommended practice.

Warm-season grasses should be dethatched shortly after the grass begins active growth. If you do it before, it may cause early green-up, with the chance of late-season frost or cold injury. Cool-season grasses should have thatch removed in the fall or early spring months when the lawn is growing vigorously. It is a good idea to reseed cool-season lawns after dethatching to promote thicker lawn coverage.

In severe thatch cases, spread removal over a two- or three-year period rather than doing it in a single operation. This will minimize stress to the lawn and invite fewer weed problems. Adequate soil moisture also makes the process much easier and less stressful to the lawn.

Core Aeration to Relieve Soil Compaction

Core aeration is primarily used to alleviate soil compaction, but it can also help remove some of the thatch layer. The aeration or coring process is performed using equipment, available for rent at tool centers and home centers, with either solid tines that poke holes in the soil, or hollow tines that pull plugs of soil from the ground, leaving them on the surface. The small holes left behind allow for better aeration and water and nutrient penetration, while relieving soil compaction.

The cores of soil on the surface can be left in place. Or you can pulverize them with a rotary mower to scatter them over the lawn. These small plugs will eventually break down, adding microorganisms and nutrients back to the soil. Coring, like dethatching, is best done when the grass is growing actively. You should use this process only when there is a serious problem such as soil compaction or excessive thatch; it is not a routine maintenance practice.

Recommended Rate for Topdressing per 1,000 Square Feet of Lawn Area:

Topdressing Thickness (Inches)	Cubic Volume	
	(Cubic Feet)	(Cubic Yards)
$1/8$	10.42	0.39
$1/4$	20.83	0.77
$5/16$	26.04	0.96
$3/8$	31.25	1.16
$1/2$	41.67	1.54
$5/8$	52.08	1.93
$3/4$	62.50	2.31
1	83.30	3.09

Topdressing

Topdressing helps reduce thatch, and also smoothes or levels the ground surface. Topdressing involves spreading a thin layer of sand, topsoil, compost, peat moss, or other organic material over the soil surface. The top-dressing comes in contact with the thatch and adds natural soil microorganisms that help break it down.

Ideally, the topdressing should be as similar as possible to the existing soil. Applying highly organic products that form distinct layers can encourage shallow roots. Suggested topdressing rates vary, but $1/2$-2 cubic yards of material per 1,000 square feet will produce a layer $1/8$-$5/8$ inch thick. If you are topdressing with heavy amounts, use multiple, light applications throughout the growing season. Drag, rake, or brush the topdressing material after it is applied so it makes good contact with the ground surface.

Supplemental fertilizer applications and a thorough watering following dethatching, coring, or topdressing will help the grass recover more quickly.

Getting Ready for Winter

Most lawns respond well to gradually raising the mowing height by $1/4$-$1/2$ inch in preparation for winter. The taller leaf blades encourage deeper root growth, and increase cold tolerance and winter protection. Also, remove tree leaves from the lawn either by raking or mowing. Many mulching mowers pulverize the leaves into small enough pieces that will quickly decompose, adding valuable organic matter back to the soil. If you are not up to the challenge of raking but don't have a mulching mower, try mowing in a diminishing circle in the same direction, blowing the leaves into a narrower pile for easier pickup by hand. You can also shred the leaves fairly well by mowing over them several times in early winter. Leaving full-sized leaves on a lawn where they will eventually pack down can not only smother the grass, allowing more weeds to get through in the spring, but can lead to cool weather diseases that attack grass stems and roots.

Instead of bagging autumn leaves and disposing of them, you can mow over them with a mulching mower. The small leaf pieces will decompose and return valuable organic material to the soil.

Protect the Environment and Get in Shape

If it is gasoline-powered, your mowing equipment impacts the environment through smog-forming emissions such as carbon monoxide and nitrogen oxide. Mowers manufactured after 1997 run 70 percent cleaner than earlier models. According to the Outdoor Power Equipment Institute, less than

Wise Mower Maintenance

Change oil seasonally

Recycle oil

Replace spark plug and air filter seasonally

Fill the gasoline tank only three-quarters full,
   allowing for heat expansion

Avoid gasoline spills

Keep blades sharp and decks clean of clippings

Review owner's manual

2 percent of smog-forming emissions come from today's lawn and garden equipment. Walk-behind, as opposed to riding, mowers contribute even smaller amounts, estimated at less than 1 percent.

Other alternatives are cordless electric or rechargeable battery-operated mowers. There are also improved reel mowers that weigh only sixteen to thirty-one pounds (compared to forty to sixty pounds for the models from years ago) and are ideal for small lawns of $1/2$ acre or less.

Did you know that when you push instead of ride, you expend as much as 450 calories per hour, which is about the same as when playing tennis or cycling? It also improves your upper-body tone and cardiovascular conditioning. Mowing the lawn or working in your garden forty-five minutes each day can lower your heart attack risk to one-third that of non-exercisers.

End of Season Care for Power Mowers

Run engine until all fuel is gone

While engine is warm, drain oil and replace with fresh oil

Clean deck

Lubricate appropriate parts

Remove battery and charge it before storage

Enjoy the break from mowing!

Low Maintenance Lawn Ideas

> *Create Curves Not Corners*
>
> *Divide and Conquer*
>
> *Group Trees Together*
>
> *Avoid Berms*
>
> *Convert High Traffic Areas*
>
> *Avoid Narrow Bands of Turf*
>
> *Create Mowing Strips*
>
> *Consider Lawn Alternatives*

Lawnscaping

Gardeners put valuable time and money into designing beds for flowers and shrubs, known as "landscaping." But for some reason, not as much consideration is given to the design and layout of the lawn. The lawn usually is more of an afterthought to quickly disguise any construction wounds. Some even believe lawn grass is easier to maintain than landscape plants. I don't know about you, but I don't spend nearly as much time grooming my annuals, perennials, and shrubs as I do my lawn plants. And that is what a lawn is—hundreds of individual plants, totaling about 850 per square foot or 8.5 million in a 10,000 square foot lawn.

Give careful thought to the best placement of these individual grass plants. Call it "lawnscaping" or "turfscaping" if it makes you feel better or brings more prestige to the activity. I just call it wise use of turf. And wise use and placement of turf can mean less time spent caring for the lawn. Isn't more free time something we would all like to have?

Curves not Corners

Flowing lines are not only pleasing to the eye, but subtle curves make mowing the lawn much easier and less time consuming. Design or replace landscape bed corners with sweeping long curves, eliminating the need to stop

Creating curved edges on your landscape beds makes for easier and quicker mowing.

and back up to cut all the grass. To lay out curves, use a water hose on the ground, and move it around until you find the design that suits you best. Drive or push your lawn mower around the edge of the hose (with the engine off, of course) to determine the easiest layout to mow. Too drastic a curve can defeat the purpose, creating even more work.

Divide and Conquer

If you are fortunate enough (or unfortunate enough, depending on your viewpoint) to have lots of space, which often translates into a large lawn, then divide and conquer. Eliminate some of the lawn, and convert it into island beds of landscape plants or outdoor art. Think about your landscape as space that needs dividing into several rooms. Walk around, and observe your space carefully and thoughtfully from different viewpoints and angles. Consider which space or room would work best for entertaining, for recreation, for growing vegetables or flowers, for storage, or for other uses you have in mind. Take into account factors such as controlling erosion, noise, and pollution, accenting your home's exterior and setting, and creating private areas of the landscape. Give some thought to how you might use different colors, shapes, and heights of landscape plants. See what those outdoor rooms might look like from indoors as well as outdoors. Think about your lawn as an anchor that ties all your outdoor rooms together and provides the foundation for recreational space.

57

Trees Mean Shade

Often outdoor rooms get planted with trees. And trees are very good things. Those small trees grow into big trees that provide wonderful shade. But to date, there is not a good lawn grass for heavy shade. So think into the future. Do you plan on hiring a professional to thin the trees carefully as they mature to give you enough light for the grass? Will you eventually remove the trees? Or do you eventually want to eliminate the grass under the tree's drip-line, replacing it with mulch or perennial shade-loving ground covers?

Group Trees Together with Mulch

If trees are planted within a reasonable distance of each other, consider getting rid of the grass entirely, and creating a cluster of trees in an island bed. A "reasonable distance" will vary from one person to another. I've done this with a cluster of three trees 18 feet apart. Forming an island bed of trees eliminates the need for mowing in and around individual trunks, which also reduces the risk of damage to the trees from the mower and weed-whacker. The space between the trees can be mulched or planted with a perennial ground cover.

Organic mulches of pine bark, wood shavings, cottonseed hulls, or recycled paper products can be used to cover space formerly occupied by grass. The mulch can be applied about 4-6 inches deep between the trees, if you aren't using ground cover plants. Avoid piling mulch against the tree trunks, since it can harbor insects and diseases. Most organic mulches decompose over time and will have to be replaced every couple of years. Many mulches are quite decorative, and they benefit the trees by retaining moisture, suppressing weeds, moderating soil temperatures, and controlling erosion.

Ground Covers Instead of Grass

There are numerous ground covers that will thrive in heavy shade where turfgrasses won't (see TABLE 5.1 in the appendix). As the ground cover spreads and matures, it will create a living mulch that prevents weeds from germinating and moderate soil temperatures. However, you will need to keep weeds and encroaching grass out until the ground cover reaches that point. Like any plants, ground covers should be selected for the appropriate cold har-

Golden Oregano

Ajuga

Perennial ground covers can be used instead of turfgrass in shady places or high traffic areas. Some good choices are ajuga, thyme, creeping jenny, golden oregano, mazus, lamium, and mondo grass.

Thyme

diness zone, soil type, soil moisture, and amount of shade. Don't forget to consider the mature height of the ground cover, which can range anywhere from a few inches to a couple of feet.

Many ground covers tolerate the heat and humidity of the South, but some melt or cook in Southern heat even in shade. If a plant likes partial shade, that usually means afternoon or dappled shade in the South. Some ground covers are invasive and can even become lawn weeds. The bottom line is to check with local experts or gardening friends to see what works best in your area.

Moss in the Lawn—Friend or Foe?

The appearance of moss in the lawn is viewed by some people as a problem. See Chapter Seven if you are one of those people and want to get rid of your moss. Moss is not able to overcome grass and so is not the villain. Instead it is an indicator of other problems. However, moss does take advantage of bare spots caused by conditions that do not favor grass. Those conditions include compacted soil, poor drainage, acidic soil, and too much shade. Instead of trying to rid your site of moss, think of it as an equally showy ornamental ground cover requiring very little fuss. Some folks go to great lengths to establish entire gardens of moss.

Mosses have no true roots, stems, flowers, fruit, or seed. They spread by spores or by sending out new shoots. Therefore, you can encourage moss to grow and spread. First, collect fragments and mix them with a small amount of water for a couple of minutes. Some gardeners use a blender, but get permission from the cook in the house first. Paint or spread the slurry in the areas where you want to encourage moss to grow.

You can also collect pieces of established moss and place them in neighboring barren areas. Make sure there is good contact with the soil. Use a nail, wire, or stake to keep the piece of moss in place until it attaches to the soil. Keep the moss well watered but not soggy. Fall or early spring is a good time to establish moss due to more abundant rainfall. It may take as many as five weeks to see any new growth. A common practice is to use buttermilk or dried skim milk to help acidify the soil and nourish the moss. A recommended rate is 1 part milk to 7 parts water. Some gardeners even suggest a one to one ratio. Apply with a hand pump sprayer, mister, or even paint the mixture on a couple of times a day for two weeks in the spring to help during the establishment period.

Berms—Oh, My!

Artificial berms, or mounds of soil above ground level, are a common design feature used to create height in an otherwise flat landscape. I've seen berms of ornamental plants and berms covered with turfgrass. I'm convinced that designers who promote berms never have had to care for the finished product. While berms may look nice to some, they are a maintenance nightmare unless their slope is very gradual. Otherwise, they are hard to mow and even harder to keep watered during drought periods. The elevated site dries out more quickly, and water runs off faster, requiring more frequent watering for shorter periods to allow the water to soak into the ground. If you want to create height, instead of constructing a berm, use landscape plants or a big boulder that doesn't need water or mowing.

High Traffic Sites

While it is true that bermuda and zoysia can take more foot traffic than most varieties of lawn grass, it is only true within reason. It is not uncommon for worn paths to appear, especially as a result of pets running back and forth frequently. Or you may be the culprit yourself, using the same route every day as a shortcut to the garden shed or the water faucet. Consider turning these high traffic areas into permanent hardscaped paths. Flagstone, brick, and concrete walkways are often expensive, but there are many other creative ways to turn worn grass paths into attractive, functional features.

The material you choose for a path should complement your overall landscape and home style. I've seen beautiful and functional walkways made of rock, treated lumber, gravel, wood chips, and even bottles buried upside down. Whatever you use, make sure you take steps to prevent grass from growing in and around the paving material, unless, of course, that is the style you want to achieve. Just keep in mind that allowing grass to grow around the hardscape minimizes the low maintenance aspects of reducing mowing and edging.

Using some type of weed block such as landscape fabric, newspaper, feed sacks, or plastic helps smother existing grass underneath the hardscape material, although weed seed can still be dropped on or blown into the path. I would suggest using such a product under your walkway unless you have chosen concrete or want to accent your path with ornamental ground cover plants. Ground covers that resist some foot traffic can be planted among rocks or other hardscape material as long as the plants match the site's light exposure. (See TABLE 5.3 in the appendix for some traffic-friendly ground covers.)

Narrow Sections of Turf— Accidents Waiting to Happen

Narrow stretches of turfgrass between the sidewalk and street are a common sight, unfortunately. Not only are these areas hard to reach with a mower or weed-eater, they can even be dangerous to maintain if you are on a street with high traffic. These sites are notorious for suffering from compacted soil, heat intensified by the concrete and asphalt, exposure to exhaust pollution, and an occasional salt application after winter ice or snowstorms. Surprisingly, many grasses do grow in these conditions, but replacing the grass with a ground cover that also will take abuse means less maintenance and less risk of injury.

Narrow strips of grass between sidewalks and landscape beds are also fairly common. Skip the grass in such small areas, and expand the landscape bed using appropriate plants and mulch.

Edging or Mowing Strips

The thought of having to use the edger or the weed-eater after I've mowed the lawn is not very appealing to me. As a matter of fact I seldom do it. Unfortunately, most of our Southern lawns spread by stolons or rhizomes, which means they are quick to invade flower or landscape beds, smothering prized ornamental plants. Routine edging or weed-eating can help keep the aggressive grasses under control, but both practices require a good bit of work and time.

"Mowing strips" can help eliminate the extra work required for edging or weed-eating. Mowing strips consist of a barrier placed between the lawn grass and the landscape bed. There are some types

Mowing Strips Along Landscape Beds

available with a flat surface designed to be positioned on the grass side of the bed for the mower tires to run on, thus allowing the mower to cut the grass bordering the strip. These strips work especially well with cool-season grasses that tend to grow in clumps. Unfortunately, mowing strips don't work well with bermuda, zoysia, or the other warm-season grasses that spread by rhizomes. These grasses just grow under, over, and around such border strips.

I have used the mowing strip principle in my own landscape to make the edging process a bit less tedious. My ornamental bed is bordered with rocks, since they are numerous and easy to come by on my acreage. They also blend nicely with our farm-style home. Instead of setting them in concrete, we lined them end to end in the soil, digging them in a little for a more natural look. But as you can imagine, mowing is all but impossible since the rock edging is very uneven.

First, I tried spraying a strip between the rocks and the grass with a herbicide. Of course, killing the grass and exposing the soil to sunlight just triggered more germinating weed seed, creating a ratty look and more work. So I experimented with using a 6-inch wide strip of cottonseed hulls about 4 inches deep as mulch between the grass and the rock border. In rural areas, cottonseed hulls are available at local farm supply or agricultural feed stores as a cattle feed, and they also work great as mulch. I have used them around landscape plants for years, and they pack nicely, don't wash or blow away easily, yet allow plenty of oxygen to reach the plant roots. I have found that I can also drive the lawn mower tires on them easily, cutting all the bordering grass with one trip.

Instead of edging or weed-eating on a weekly basis, I spot treat with a herbicide as soon as the bermudagrass starts to grow over or through the mulch barrier. I only have to do this once or twice a month, which has been a big time saver. The cottonseed hull barrier outside the rock edging also adds a finishing curve that looks attractive.

Of course, you can use the same method with bricks, flagstone, concrete, or any product that will support the weight of the mower tires. Just remember that most warm-season grasses will still have to be managed to stop them from creeping into your flower or landscape beds.

You can use this same technique to control grass adjoining sidewalks and driveways. Instead of spraying herbicide to kill the strip of grass bordering the concrete or asphalt, wait and spray the runners when they start to grow over the hard surface. Exposing bare soil in the lawn increases weeds, and the narrow band of dead grass is unsightly as well.

Turf Varieties

> **Understand Warm- and Cool-Season Grasses**
>
> **Match Grass to Growing Area and Soil Type**
>
> **Consider Personal Preferences**
>
> **Be Aware of Time Needed for Maintenance**
>
> **Research Availability of Varieties**
>
> **Look for Improved Pest-Resistant Cultivars**

Selection of Grasses

It is very important to select the appropriate lawn variety for your growing area. While cold hardiness is not as big an issue with turfgrass as with ornamental plants, it is a major factor in the transition zone between cool-season and warm-season grasses. There are optimum locations for each grass variety grown in the South, as shown on the state map in the Introduction, based not only on winter temperatures, but on summer heat, soil structure and pH, drainage, and rainfall. It is certainly possible to grow a grass variety outside its optimum location, particularly if you have a microclimate that suits the variety well, but it is more risky than growing a type that prefers your region. The easiest and most conservative approach is to observe the grass varieties growing successfully in your area, then select available, improved cultivars when establishing or renovating your lawn.

There are your personal plans and preferences to consider, such as the texture of the leaf blades, the amount of foot traffic anticipated, your willingness to provide supplemental irrigation, retail availability, and the amount of time you are prepared to devote to lawn care. Additional considerations in choosing a variety include its tolerance to pests and diseases. This will be influenced by the amount of care given; too much care, as well as too little, can magnify problems. Unfortunately, there is no such thing as a perfect, no-maintenance grass. You will need to consider the pros and cons of each variety based on your own expectations.

Keep in mind that seeding more heavily than recommended, or spacing plugs and sprigs closer together, can help give you quicker coverage when establishing a new lawn.

Table 6.1

Warm-Season Turfgrass Comparisons

Characteristics	Bermuda	Carpet	Centipede	St. Augustine	Zoysia
Growing Height	$1/2$- 2 inches	1-2 inches	1-2 inches	2-3 inches	$3/4$ -$1^1/2$ in.
Soil pH	5.5-6.9	4.5-5.9	5.0-6.5	5.5-7.0	5.5-6.9
Drought Tolerance	excellent	fair	fair	fair	fair
Salt Tolerance	good	poor	poor	good	fair
Partial Shade Tolerance	poor	fair	fair	good	fair
Heat Tolerance	excellent	excellent	excellent	excellent	excellent
Cold Tolerance	good	poor	good	fair	excellent
Cold Hardiness Zones	6a – 9b	8b – 9b	7a – 9b	7b – 9b	6a – 9b
Wear Tolerance	excellent	fair	poor	fair	excellent
Spreading Rate	fast	slow	moderate	fast	slow
Color	dark	medium	light	dark	dark
Texture	fine	coarse	medium	coarse	fine

Table 6.2

Cool-Season Turfgrass Comparisons

Characteristics	Kentucky Bluegrass	Tall Fescue
Growing Height	2-3 inches	2-3 inches
Soil pH	6.0-7.0	5.5-7.0
Drought Tolerance	fair	poor
Salt Tolerance	poor	fair
Partial Shade Tolerance	fair	good
Heat Tolerance	poor	fair
Cold Tolerance	excellent	excellent
Cold Hardiness Zones	6a – 6b	6a – 7b
Wear Tolerance	fair	fair
Spreading Rate	moderate	not applicable
Color	dark	dark
Texture	medium	coarse

Bermudagrass
(Wiregrass, Couchgrass, Devilgrass)
Cynodon dactylon and hybrids

Bermudagrass is a native of Africa and was introduced to the U.S. in the mid-1700s primarily as a pasture and forage grass. Bermuda was first used for lawns and sports fields in the 1920s. Bermudagrass is most often categorized as either common or a hybrid selection. Common bermuda, also known as 'Arizona Common', is one of the earliest seeded cultivars used and has grown its way into the Southeast as the primary turfgrass species. 'Arizona Common' is a tough grass, but not quite as cold hardy as some of its improved counterparts. It also doesn't produce the thick layer of turf most people prefer for their lawns.

The new and improved hybrids are selections bred for better lawn qualities. Some cultivars are available by seed, but many of the hybrids are sterile and available only in vegetative forms such as sprigs, plugs, or sod. All spread either by rhizomes or stolons. Some of the newer selections, known as "fairway" or "putting green" types, are better for golf courses than home lawns because of their fine, compact growth habit requiring intensive maintenance. All bermudagrass foliage is sensitive to cold. The grass quickly gets a green and golden mottled appearance after the first frost. Top growth will stop when day and night temperatures begin to average 50° F. The roots keep growing after the leaf blades go dormant and continue to grow until the ground temperature reaches near freezing or colder. As the temperatures warm up the following spring, the grass resumes normal growth.

Bermudagrass

Facts

Warm-Season Grass

Growing Height – $1/2$-2 inches

Mow When Grass Reaches – $3/4$-3 inches

Soil pH – 5.5-6.9

Drought Tolerance – excellent

Salt Tolerance – good

Tolerance of Partial Shade – poor

Heat Tolerance – excellent

Cold Tolerance – good

Cold Hardiness Zones – 6a-9b

Wear Tolerance – excellent

Spreading Rate – fast

Color – dark green

Texture – fine

Planting Methods

Seeding Rate – hulled seed 1-2 lbs. per 1,000 sq. ft., non-hulled seed 3-5 lbs. per 1,000 sq. ft. for new lawns

Overseeding Rate – $1/2$ lb. hulled and 2 lbs. non-hulled per 1,000 sq. ft. for established, thinning lawns

Vegetative Planting Rate – 3-10 bushels sprigs per 1,000 sq. ft. for 6-12 in. spacing

3-12+ yards of sod per 1,000 sq. ft. to make 2-inch plugs spaced 6 to 12 inches apart

Divide total square footage of lawn by 9 to figure yards of sod needed.

Optimum Planting Time – April-June

Advantages

Wide pH range

Drought tolerant

Marginal salt tolerance

Greater turf density (hybrids)

Disease tolerance (hybrids)

Fine texture

Favorable color

Fewer seed heads (hybrids)

Excellent wear tolerance

Disadvantages

Unsightly seed head (common bermuda)

Cold hardiness (some varieties)

Landscape weed

Goes dormant or brown in the winter

Very poor shade tolerance

Primary Pests

Insects: Armyworm, Bermuda Mite, Billbug, Chinchbug, Cutworm, Ground Pearl, Mealybug, Mole Cricket, Sod Webworm, Spittlebug, White Grub

Diseases: Brown Patch, Dollar Spot, Leaf Spot

Other: Nematodes, Spring Dead Spot

See the appendix for a list of cultivars.

Carpetgrass
(Flatgrass, Louisianagrass)
Axonopus affinis

Carpetgrass is often confused with and compared to St. Augustinegrass because of its coarse leaf blades, creeping habit, and Southern history. The leaf blade tips are more blunt and rounded than St. Augustine, and they emerge from the grass stem at a 45° angle. St. Augustine's angle of emergence is closer to 90°. Carpetgrass spreads primarily by seed and stolons, making a dense, thick lawn. It is easy to start from seed. The seed stalks resemble crabgrass and elongate more and faster than St. Augustine, reaching some 10-15 inches tall if not mowed. During the growing season the quickly emerging seed heads make frequent mowing necessary.

Carpetgrass is not nearly as cold hardy as St. Augustine and thrives in poor, wet, acidic, sandy soils along the Gulf Coast. Carpetgrass will tolerate some shade but not nearly as much as St. Augustinegrass. It is not appealing to most homeowners as a lawn grass unless they have a very specific wet, acidic site (with a pH range of 4.5-5.9), with poor soil. Since it can endure and prosper in low fertility sites, carpetgrass is also used in areas requiring a low-maintenance turfgrass. The cultivar 'Chase' is available. A close relative, *Axonopus compressus*, also known as tropical carpetgrass, is not cold hardy and does not work as well as a lawn grass.

Carpetgrass

Facts

Warm-Season Grass

Growing Height – 1-2 inches

Mow When Grass Reaches – 1½-3 inches

Soil pH – 4.5-5.9

Drought Tolerance – fair

Salt Tolerance – poor

Tolerance of Partial Shade – fair

Heat Tolerance – excellent

Cold Tolerance – poor

Cold Hardiness Zones – 8b-9b

Wear Tolerance – fair

Spreading Rate – slow

Color – medium green

Texture – coarse

Advantages

Grows in moist sites

Prefers acidic soils

Low fertility requirements

Easy to start from seed

Disadvantages

Rapidly emerging seed stalk

Poor cold hardiness

Planting Methods

Seeding Rate – 1-3 lbs. per 1,000 sq. ft. for new lawns

Overseeding Rate – 4-5 lbs. per 1,000 sq. ft. for established, thinning lawns

Vegetative Planting Rate – 2-4 bushels of sprigs per 1,000 sq. ft. for 6-12 in. spacing

3-12+ yards of sod per 1,000 sq. ft. to make 2 in. plugs spaced 6 to 12 inches

Divide total square footage of lawn by 9 to figure yards of sod needed.

Optimum Planting Time – March-May

Primary Pests

Insects:	Armyworm
	Cutworm
	White Grub
	Mole Cricket
	Sod Webworm
Diseases:	Brown Patch
	Dollar Spot
	Leaf Spot
	Pythium Blight
Other:	Nematodes

Centipedegrass
(Chinagrass or Chinesegrass)
Eremochloa ophiuroides

Centipedegrass, a native of Southeast Asia, is favored by many home-owners in the South because it is known as a low maintenance grass. As a matter of fact, if you give it too much tender loving care you can harm it. It does not require frequent mowing unless you over-fertilize. It is naturally a light yellow-green color. Foliar iron applications can help generate a greener color, but it will last only a couple of mowings. Nitrogen fertilizer applications can also increase the green color. If over-applied, however, nitrogen can lead centipede to decline, eventually harming the grass.

Centipede spreads by seed and vegetatively. Its short, upright stolons resemble centipedes, thus the name. Since its stolons run along the soil sur-face rather than underground, and it is slower growing, it is easier to keep from invading flower beds than bermudagrass is. It is more tolerant of shade than bermuda, but not by much, so don't use it in a shady area. It will grow in poor soils that are slightly acidic. It is fairly cold hardy, although it is sub-ject to winter kill if temperatures drop suddenly, and it can occasionally be found growing outside its optimum region in protected microclimates. Centipede is primarily started by seed but is also available as plugs or sod. The seed is quite slow to germinate. In coastal areas, centipedegrass can remain somewhat green during mild winters.

Centipedegrass

Facts

Warm-Season Grass

Growing Height – 1-2 inches

Mow When Grass Reaches –
1¹/₂-3 inches

Soil pH – 5.0-6.5

Drought Tolerance – fair

Salt Tolerance – poor

Partial Shade Tolerance – fair

Heat Tolerance – excellent

Cold Tolerance – good

Cold Hardiness Zones – 7a-9b

Wear Tolerance – poor

Spreading Rate – moderate

Color – light green

Texture – medium

Advantages

Responds to minimal care

Grows slowly

Disadvantages

Sensitive to salt

Grows slowly

Yellowish color

In colder winters blades turn
brown

Iron deficiency in alkaline soils

Planting Methods

Seeding Rate – ¹/₄-1 lb. per 1,000 sq.
ft. for new lawns

Overseeing Rate – ¹/₂ lb. per
1,000 sq. ft. for established,
thinning lawns

Vegetative Planting Rate –
2-4 bushels of sprigs per 1,000 sq.
ft. for 6-12 in. spacing

3-12+ yards of sod per 1,000 sq. ft.
to make 2 in. plugs spaced 6 to
12 inches

Divide total square footage of lawn
by 9 to figure yards of sod needed.

Optimum Planting Time – April-June

Primary Pests

Insects: Billbug

Chinch Bug

Ground Pearl

Mole Cricket

Sod Webworm

Spittlebug

White Grub

Diseases: Brown Patch

Dollar Spot

Other: Centipede Decline

Nematodes

See the appendix for a list of cultivars.

St. Augustinegrass
(Charlestongrass)
Stenotaphrum secundatum

St. Augustine is one of the most shade tolerant of all Southern grasses. It is used successfully as a lawn grass among tall pines in many landscape settings. Even so, it will not perform well in dense, heavy shade. This coarse-leaved grass with its blue-green color can make a beautiful lawn, especially if mowed at a higher setting. St. Augustinegrass is well suited to the warm humid conditions of the Deep South. It is tropical in origin and native to the Americas, West Africa, and the Pacific Islands.

Unfortunately, it requires diligent monitoring for pests. Careful thought and research should go into selecting new cultivars that are pest and disease resistant. It is particularly sensitive to chinch bug and St. Augustine decline virus (SADV). Do not over-fertilize with nitrogen, which can increase pest problems. St. Augustine grown outside its preferred locations may be killed in winter, although more cold hardy selections are being released. Consistent winter temperatures around 16-20° F can damage St. Augustinegrass. The grass spreads by stolons, and seed when allowed to mature.

St. Augustinegrass

Facts

Warm-Season Grass

Growing Height – 2-3 inches (or higher if mower settings will allow)

Mow When Grass Reaches – 3-4$^1/_4$ inches

Soil pH – 5.5-7.0

Drought Tolerance – fair

Salt Tolerance – good

Tolerance of Partial Shade – good

Heat Tolerance – excellent

Cold Tolerance – fair

Cold Hardiness Zones – 7b-9b

Wear Tolerance – fair

Spreading Rate – fast

Color – dark green

Texture – coarse

Advantages

Dark green color

Coarse leaf blade

Tolerant of salt

Tolerant of partial shade

Disadvantages

Pest prone

Marginal cold hardiness

Dormant brown winter color

Planting Methods

Seeding Rate – $^1/_3$-$^1/_2$ lb. per 1,000 sq. ft. (very few cultivars available as seed)

Vegetative Planting Rate –
2-4 bushels of sprigs per 1,000 sq. ft. for 6-12 inch spacing

3-12+ yards of sod per 1,000 sq. ft. to make 2 inch plugs spaced 6 to 12 inches

Divide total square footage of lawn by 9 to figure yards of sod needed.

Optimum Planting Time – April-June

Primary Pests

Insects:	Armyworm
	Chinch Bug
	Ground Pearl
	Mealybug
	Mole Cricket
	Sod Webworm
	Spittlebug
Diseases:	Brown Patch
	Downy Mildew
	Gray Leaf Spot
Other:	Nematodes
	St. Augustine Decline

See the appendix for a list of cultivars.

Zoysiagrass

Zoysia species

Z oysia, a native of Southeast Asia, is cherished by many as the ideal lawn grass because of its fine leaf blades and thick, carpet-like growth. It is also touted as one of the most high maintenance turfgrass varieties, yet I have seen beautiful zoysia lawns that receive minimal fertilizer and care. Over-fertilizing and over-watering can easily lead to thatch problems with zoysia. In any case, it requires consistent and routine mowing at the recommended cutting heights. Zoysia also responds well to the use of reel mowers, which many experts highly recommend. However, the cultivar 'El Toro' has been developed for mowing with a rotary mower. Zoysia is relatively slow to establish and can be started with seed, sprigs, plugs, or sod depending on the cultivar. Research shows that a topdressing applied over newly set sprigs helps increase sprig survival and leads to quicker establishment. Zoysia is more shade tolerant than bermudagrass and centipedegrass, but not as tolerant as Kentucky bluegrass and fescue. It has good wear tolerance but is slower to recuperate from damage than bermuda. Zoysia spreads by rhizomes and stolons.

Zoysia species include the cold tolerant *Z. japonica* (Japanese or Korean lawngrass or common zoysia); *Z. matrella* (Manilagrass); *Z. tenuifolia* (Korean velvetgrass or mascarenegrass), which is less cold hardy and best for coastal areas only; and *Z. sinica* (seashoregrass). There are cultivars available of these species, and hybrids.

Zoysiagrass

Facts

Warm-Season Grass

Growing Height – $3/4$-$1^1/2$ inches

Mow When Grass Reaches –
$1^1/8$-$2^1/4$ inches

Soil pH – 5.5-6.9

Drought Tolerance – fair

Salt Tolerance – fair

Partial Shade Tolerance – fair

Heat Tolerance – excellent

Cold Tolerance – excellent

Cold Hardiness Zones – 6a-9b

Wear Tolerance – excellent

Spreading Rate – slow

Color – dark green

Texture – fine

Planting Methods

Seeding Rate – 2-4 lbs. per 1,000 sq. ft. for new lawns

Vegetative Planting Rate –
2-4 bushels of sprigs per 1,000 sq. ft. for 6-12 in. spacing

3-12+ yards of sod per 1,000 sq. ft. to make 2 in. plugs spaced 6-12 inches

Divide total square footage of lawn by 9 to figure yards of sod needed.

Optimum Planting Time – April-June

Advantages

Golf course appearance

Slow growing

Disadvantages

Thatch problems with improper care

Slower to cover after planting

More costly to establish

Dormant brown winter color

Primary Pests

Insects: Armyworm

Billbug

Cutworm

Ground Pearl

Sod Webworm

White Grub

Diseases: Brown Patch

Dollar Spot

Leaf Spot

Rust

Other: Nematodes

See the appendix for a list of cultivars.

Chapter Six

Kentucky Bluegrass

Poa pratensis

Traveling the northern United States oftentimes tempts Southern gardeners to want to try Northern plants at home. Kentucky bluegrass, a beautiful cool-season grass, is no exception. If you want to try it in the South though, it is best grown at higher elevations or in the northernmost counties in the transition zone between cool- and warm-season regions. The lovely color and relatively slow growth rate make for a wonderful lawn, but Kentucky bluegrass cannot tolerate the heat and humidity of the Deep South. Kentucky bluegrass also needs a bit more water than warm-season grasses, though it can survive a drought better than might be expected, even when allowed to go dormant. Kentucky bluegrass is a native of Europe and northern Asia, and might have come to North America with the early colonists.

Kentucky bluegrass is somewhat shade tolerant in the South, but will take less shade than its cool-season counterpart, tall fescue. It spreads by rhizomes but not nearly as vigorously as bermuda or zoysia. Kentucky bluegrass prefers a slightly acid pH. There are numerous cultivars available on the market. A blend of two or more is recommended, since different varieties exhibit different levels of tolerance for pests and adverse environmental conditions.

Kentucky Bluegrass

Facts

Cool-Season Grass

Growing Height – 2-3 inches

Mow When Grass Reaches – 3-4$\frac{1}{4}$ inches

Soil pH – 6.0-7.0

Drought Tolerance – fair

Salt Tolerance – poor

Tolerance of Partial Shade – fair

Heat Tolerance – poor

Cold Tolerance – excellent

Cold Hardiness Zones – 6a-6b

Wear Tolerance – fair

Spreading Rate – moderate

Color – dark green

Texture – medium

Advantages

Nice color

Not invasive

Tolerant of partial shade

Disadvantages

Not heat tolerant

Disease problems in South

Planting Methods

Seeding Rate – 2-3 lbs. per 1,000 sq. ft. for new lawns

Overseeding Rate – 1$\frac{1}{2}$ lbs. per 1,000 sq. ft. for established, thinning lawns

Vegetative Planting Rates – Sprigging is seldom done because it is easier and cheaper to start from seed. If sprigs are found, use 2-4 bushels of sprigs per 1,000 sq. ft. for 6-12 in. spacing. Use 3-12+ yards of sod per 1,000 sq. ft. to make 2 inch plugs spaced 6 to 12 inches. Divide total square footage of lawn by 9 to figure yards of sod needed.

Optimum Planting Time – Late September-October, or March-April

Primary Pests

Insects:	Armyworm
	Billbug
	Cutworm
	Sod Webworm
	White Grub
Diseases:	Brown Patch
	Gray Leaf Spot
	Rust
	Powdery Mildew
	Fusarium Blight
Other:	Nematodes

See the appendix for a list of cultivars.

Tall Fescue

Festuca arundinacea

Tall Fescue is a cool-season grass that will tolerate the upper and mid-South as long as supplemental irrigation can be provided during the summer. It will not perform well in the lower South or in coastal areas. It is tolerant of partial shade, which can help keep it from going completely dormant in the heat of the summer. Fescue grows best in spring and fall. It is a clumping grass (with no rhizomes or stolons) and requires overseeding every couple of seasons to keep the grass thick. The coarse blades respond best to a higher mower setting, often as high as the mower will go, especially if grown in shade. This encourages deep roots needed to thrive in the summer heat.

Fescue is quite cold hardy and is best adapted along the northern tier of Southern states in the transition zone between cool-season and warm-season grasses. It remains green throughout the winter if temperatures are mild. In severe winters, it is normal for the grass blades to burn and turn brown. Once temperatures warm, the grass quickly begins to green up and grow. The most commonly grown fescue, 'K-31', is actually a pasture forage grass that has made its way into many lawns. There are many new improved cultivars that out-perform 'K-31'. These are often referred to as "turf-type" selections. Some have finer blades and are more compact. Fescue is quite susceptible to foliage diseases in the South, thanks in part to the high humidity. As a result, experts suggest mixing one or more cultivars together when planting a fescue lawn.

Tall Fescue

Facts

Cool-Season Grass

Growing Height – 2-3 inches (or higher if mower settings will allow)

Mow Grass When Reaches – 3-4$\frac{1}{4}$ inches

Soil pH – 5.5-7.0

Drought Tolerance – poor

Salt Tolerance – fair

Tolerance of Partial Shade – good

Heat Tolerance – fair

Cold Tolerance – excellent

Cold Hardiness Zones – 6a-7b

Wear Tolerance – fair

Spreading Rate – not applicable since fescue grows in clumps

Color – dark green

Texture – coarse

Advantages

Tolerance of partial shade

Not invasive

Grows rapidly

Disadvantages

Not drought tolerant

Low tolerance for heat

Grows rapidly

Planting Methods

Seeding Rate – 7-10 lbs. per 1,000 sq. ft. for new lawns

Overseeding Rate – 3-6 lbs. per 1,000 sq. ft. for established, thinning lawns

Vegetative Planting Rate – sod only, sprigging and plugging not recommended

Optimum Planting Time – Late September-October, March-April

Primary Pests

Insects:	Armyworm
	Cutworm
	White Grub
Diseases:	Brown Patch
	Fusarium Blight
	Gray Leaf Spot
	Pythium Blight
Other:	Nematodes

See the appendix for a list of cultivars.

Fine-leaved fescues are predominantly Northern grasses but occasionally show up in the South in seed mixes. These include creeping red fescue, *Festuca rubra*, chewing fescue, *F. rubra* var. *commutata*, and hard fescue, *F. longifolia*. These grasses are not as tolerant of the heat and humidity of the South as the coarser "turf-type" fescues. They are also more prone to diseases in the South. Like many of the cool-season grasses grown in the South, they will tolerate partially shaded sites but may never perform up to your expectations as a lawn grass.

Red Fescue—spreading growth habit with underground rhizomes or stems, more shade and drought tolerant, but not nearly as heat tolerant, as other fescues. Often mixed with Kentucky bluegrass seed. Keep at around $1^1/2$-2 inches, mow when $2^1/4$-3 inches. Cultivars include 'Ambassador', 'Boreal', 'Flyer', 'Jasper', Pernille', and 'Red Ruby'.

Chewing Fescue—resembles tall fescue, though more drought and shade tolerant, and not as tolerant of wear and heat. Has clumping growth and can be mowed closer. Keep at around 2-$2^1/2$ inches, mow when 3-$3^3/4$ inches. Cultivars include 'Atlanta', 'Banner', 'Jamestown', 'Tiffany', 'Treasure', and 'Victory'.

Hard Fescue—grows in clumps similar to tall fescue but has a finer texture, tolerates dry shade. Keep at around 2-$2^1/2$ inches, mow when 3-$3^3/4$ inches. Cultivars include 'Aurora', 'Bighorn', 'Brigade', 'Discovery', and 'Nordic'.

Other Grass Varieties to Know

Bahiagrass

Like it or not, bahiagrass, *Paspalum notatum*, has made a name for itself in the lawn industry, mostly as a weed. It is a native of South America and was introduced to the U.S. as a pasture or roadside grass. Bahiagrass has a signature "V" shaped seed head, and can spread quite readily in milder portions of the Southeast, invading other prized Southern turfgrasses. It is also quite aggressive thanks to an extensive root system that enables it to overcome other grasses under stress from drought. At the same time, some of those same characteristics make it a good turfgrass. The most frustrating maintenance consideration is the speed with which the seed head arises after mowing. Bahiagrass spreads by seed and rhizome, but it does not always fill in thickly to make a dense lawn. Therefore, occasional overseeding will be required. Bahia prefers warmer sub-tropical and tropical climates and is best adapted to sandy, slightly acidic, infertile soils. Cultivars include 'Argentine', 'Paraguay', 'Pensacola', 'Tifton-9', and 'Wilmington'.

Buffalograss

Buffalograss, *Buchloe dactyloides*, is a North American Great Plains native thriving in neutral or alkaline soils. It performs best in the semi-arid regions of Texas and Oklahoma. Buffalograss is relatively slow growing and requires minimal mowing depending on fertility and rainfall. In some situations, it doesn't have to be mowed at all, creating a soft, wavy, tufted appearance, reaching a height of 6-8 inches. In such cases, the grass should not be fertilized and seldom watered. Avoid over-fertilizing and overwatering buffalograss in any case, or it will decline. Buffalograss should be mowed when it reaches $3-4^{1}/_{4}$ inches, to maintain a height of 2-3 inches.

Buffalograss spreads by stolons and occasionally by seed. There are separate male and female flowers. The male flowers shoot up quickly after mowing, forming seed heads or "flags" that are not always preferred in a lawn setting. As a result, new all-female types are being introduced into the turf trade. Buffalograss is available by seed or vegetatively. The so-called "seed" is actually a burr containing several individual seeds. Deburred seed is harder to find and quite expensive. The seed should be planted deeper than most turfgrass at about $^{1}/_{2}$ inch. It can take several weeks for the seed to germinate. The seeding rate is 1-3 lbs. per 1,000 square feet, or 4-6 lbs. per 1,000 square feet for faster coverage of new lawns. Plugs and sod are also methods of establishment. Sprigs are seldom available because of the stoloniferous, above-ground growth habit of buffalograss. The vegetative planting rate is 12 yards or more of sod per 1,000 square feet, to make 2-inch plugs spaced 6 inches apart. Cultivars include 'Bison', 'Cody', 'Comanche', 'Plains', 'Sharp's Improved', 'Tantanka', 'Texoka', and 'Topgun' (available as seed); and '318', '378', '609', 'Buffalawn', 'Legacy', 'Midget', 'Mobuff', 'Prairie', and 'Stampede' (available in vegetative forms).

Gramagrass

No, "grama" doesn't have anything to do with the way we Southerners talk, but instead refers to a couple of prairie grasses called blue grama, *Bouteloua gracilis*, and sideoats grama, *Bouteloua curtipendula*. These native Plains grasses are quite cold hardy and prefer the same growing conditions as buffalograss. In other words, they don't like the humid, wet conditions of the Southeast. Instead, they thrive in the heavy soils of the Southwestern arid locales of Oklahoma and Texas.

Blue grama tends to have a fine leaf and is a light green, bunching grass, which is a nice alternative to the typical spreading, somewhat invasive warm-season selections. Of course, that also means occasional reseeding to keep a nice turf appearance. Blue grama is occasionally mixed with buffalograss seed for a prairie warm-season mix, and it is somewhat easier to establish than buffalo.

Sideoats grama is a light gray-green color with coarser leaves, also clumping in growth habit and very easy to establish from seed. If allowed to mature and set seed, it has unique seed heads that emerge in a zig-zag pattern, making for an interesting ornamental landscape grass.

Improved lawn selections are still in the works, but the ones to date make great choices for prairie restoration and landscaping sites that require minimal mowing. Both species are very drought tolerant once established. Improved cultivars to date for blue grama are 'Hachita' and 'Bad River Ecotype'; good cultivars of sideoats grama include 'Kildeer', 'Pierre', and 'Butte'.

Rough Bluegrass

Rough bluegrass, *Poa trivialis*, also known as rough stalk meadowgrass, is also used as an annual cool-season grass on warm-season lawns. This small-seeded grass is particularly good for overseeding lawns such as zoysia and bermuda since it is tolerant of partial shade and does not make a thick dense sod. It is very winter hardy and should be maintained around 2-2$^{1}/_{2}$ inches or mowed when it reaches 3-3$^{3}/_{4}$ inches. The color is close to apple green. The recommended overseeding rate is 4-7 lbs. per 1,000 square feet. Rough bluegrass is sometimes combined with Kentucky bluegrass seed in mixes. Avoid this combination if possible in the cooler, high elevation growing zones—the rough bluegrass can potentially live through the summer, overtaking the Kentucky bluegrass.

Ryegrass

Ryegrass is a cool-season grass and a common sight in the South during the winter. It does not perform well as a permanent grass in the South, but it is widely used to overseed dormant warm-season grasses to give lawns green winter color. It has a clumping growth habit and does not develop rhizomes or stolons. Care must be taken though, since continued overseeding can create competition for the underlying warm-season grass and reduce its coverage.

Ryegrass is available as an annual, *Lolium multiflorum*, or as a perennial, *Lolium perenne*. Most folks overseed with the annual variety, since it is typically cheaper and germinates faster. Perennial ryegrass will also work for overseeding since it usually does not live through hot, humid Southern summers. It has darker green color, finer texture, and better turf quality than the annual species. Both are somewhat tolerant of partial shade.

Intermediate ryegrass, *Lolium hybridum*, is a fairly new type that is a cross between annual ryegrass and perennial ryegrass. Intermediates are alternatives for overseeding bermudagrass because they die out earlier, resulting in less potential harm to the warm-season grass. There are new hybrid intermediate cultivars being developed, and they are typically cheaper than perennial ryegrass. 'Interim', 'Froghair', and 'Transist' are some of the earliest releases. The green color of these selections is somewhat lighter than perennial ryegrass and darker than annual cultivars. The leaf blades are also finer than annual ryegrass. Mowing height and care are the same.

Use 8-12 lbs. of seed per 1,000 square feet for seeding over existing warm-season grass in late fall. Overseeding can be done two to four weeks before the average first frost date or shortly thereafter.

Green winter color also means winter mowing. The grass height should be maintained at about 2-2^1/$_2$ inches, which means it needs mowing when it reaches 3-3^3/$_4$ inches. Be careful not to use high nitrogen fertilizers on ryegrass or it can cause the dormant warm-season grass to green up out of season and be more susceptible to winter injury. A fertilizer analysis with 10 percent nitrogen is best.

Seashore Paspalum

Seashore paspalum, *Paspalum vaginatum*, is a warm-season grass, native to tropical and subtropical regions of North and South America, that is not used widely in the U.S. to date. But with time, research, and more exposure, it may well become a major contender as a Southern lawn grass. It is often compared to bermuda because of its fine texture and growth habit. It is also about as shade tolerant as bermuda, which is basically not at all. But that is as far as the comparisons go.

Seashore paspalum is very tolerant of salt, wet sites, and a variety of soils. It will thrive in soils with a pH range of 3.6-10 and will grow in sand, heavy clay, mucks, or bogs. It is tolerant of heavy foot traffic. It doesn't need heavy applications of fertilizer to keep its appearance. The grass should be maintained at about $1/2$-1 inch, and mowed when it reaches $3/4$-1 $1/2$ inches. If it is over-fertilized and over-watered, seashore paspalum can develop thatch.

Seashore paspalum is not quite as cold hardy as bermuda, and its optimum growing region is similar to that of centipedegrass. Seashore paspalum tends to green up from its winter dormancy a little later than most warm-season lawns but doesn't turn brown after the first frost as quickly. Cultivars are being developed for greater cold tolerance. It can also be overseeded with cool-season grasses for winter color. And it can be fairly drought tolerant once established.

Seashore paspalum is often touted as the perfect grass for the 21st century because of its tolerance to seawater and recycled non-potable wastewater. It is even being tested for its effectiveness in cleaning up contaminated soils. To date, there are no serious pest problems other than the pests common to Southern lawns.

Because of its wide range of adaptability, seashore paspalum makes a nice choice for roadways, sports fields, and lawns. There are several named cultivars on the market to date, including 'Saltene', 'Salpas', 'Futurf', 'Adalayd', 'Excalibur', 'Tropic Shore', 'Salam', 'Sea Isle', 'Durban', and 'Country Club'. The leaf blade textures vary among cultivars from very fine to more coarse. Seashore paspalum has a dark green, almost lustrous, shiny appearance resulting from a waxy covering that also repels morning dew quite nicely.

While it sounds like the perfect lawn grass, seashore paspalum requires proper management and regular mowing and care, just as any turfgrass does. Thus far, it is not widely available and is somewhat expensive. Since seashore paspalum is so new and underused, there are few pest and weed control products labeled for use on it.

There are many turfgrass options available. When choosing a grass for your lawn, consider your regional conditions, your particular site, availability at local stores, personal preferences in grass texture and appearance, anticipated use of the lawn, maintenance requirements, and pest resistance.

Common Turfgrass Pests

Chapter Seven

> **Figure Out Whether the Problem Is Insect, Disease, Weed, or Other**
>
> **Be Observant for Changes in Your Lawn**
>
> **Watch for Symptoms and Signs**
>
> **Gauge the Proper Time for Action**
>
> **Use a Process of Elimination to Identify the Problem**
>
> **Follow Good Management Practices as the First Line of Defense**
>
> **Spot Treat if Possible**
>
> **Use Chemicals as a Last Resort**

If only we could grow a lawn and not have to deal with pests! Nice thought, but that "ain't gonna happen." Not only is the South home to very friendly and cordial folks, it's also home to some very neighborly pests, and I'm not talking about your neighbor who keeps tabs on how well your lawn looks. There are weeds, insects, diseases, and other annoying problems that can wreak havoc on your little green oasis, better known as a lawn.

The following sections will help you identify some of the most common pests and determine how to manage them. The first step is to lose the word "eradicate" from your vocabulary. Mother Nature intends for us to all coexist. And just about the time you think you have gotten rid of that pesky weed or bug, Mother Nature shows you who is in control by introducing something else. Remember that your lawn, garden, and landscape all make up a living ecology and work together, not independently of each other. What you do to one affects the others.

Be observant, be patient, and realize there are alternatives to chemicals. Many times, a simple change in a management practice can correct the problem or allow natural predators or beneficial insects to do their job. It is all a matter of perspective. A few weeds aren't the end of a beautiful lawn. As a matter of fact, they may well be the beginning of a healthy ecosystem in your yard.

Some weeds even attract birds and beneficial insects. The key is learning to identify which pests or problems cause only minor damage that you can live with, and which ones need more attention, but can be controlled with beneficial or organic measures before you bring in the chemicals.

Diagnosing Pest Problems

Process of Elimination

If the cause of a pest problem is not immediately obvious, you need to follow a process of elimination. Answering these questions can help. Many of these topics have been addressed in detail earlier in this book.

- *What are the specific symptoms? Be observant, dig, pull, and look from different directions.*

- *Does the problem have a distinct pattern to it? Small independent circles? Large complete circle? Irregular appearance? Streaked appearance? Or no distinct shape at all?*

- *Is the problem in one spot or over the entire lawn?*

- *Do individual leaf blades have spots, distinctively shaped lesions, or streaked areas?*

- *Are the roots healthy with abundant, white, fibrous roots? If not, are they stunted, slimy, or chewed? Do they have holes in them or are they an obvious color?*

- *How long has the problem been present?*

- *Did the problem seem to appear overnight? If so when was the last time you were out in your yard?*

- *What is your specific type of lawn grass? Some are more prone to certain problems.*

- *When was the last time you fertilized? What did you use and how much?*

- *Have you ever taken a soil test? If so, when was the last time?*

- *Have you probed the area to see if your soil is hard or compacted?*

- *What is your mowing height?*

- *Did you check for buried foreign material such as sand, nails, limestone, etc. in the problem area?*

- *When was the last time you sharpened or changed your mower blade?*

- *When and how often do you water?*

- *Is there a thatch layer? If so, how thick?*

- *What time of year is it? Spring, summer, fall, or winter?*

- *Is there a drought occurring? High heat or humidity?*

- *Has there been an abundance of rainfall?*

- *Was there a recent light frost?*

- *What is your soil type or structure? Sand, clay, silt, or loam?*

- *Have you ever topdressed your lawn? If so, with what?*

- *Does your soil drain well?*

- *Is the problem in shade, partial shade, or sun?*

- *Have you spilled something in that spot recently? Oil, gas, fertilizer, paint cleaner, or something similar?*

- *Have you drained a swimming pool in that area?*

- *Is the area near a septic tank or sewer drainage line?*

Troubleshooting Symptoms

Scenario 1 – Grass affected in distinct circular patterns:

Symptoms	Possible Causes
Center dead, yellowish-brown grass	Chinch Bugs
Yellowish-brown color mixed with healthy grass	Brown Patch
Grass brown or wilted, easily pulls up, roots and all	Mole Crickets
Dark green pattern, mushrooms outside circle	Fairy Ring
Spots grayish green to brown, leaves rolled, dry soil	Drought
Leaves chewed	Armyworms
Yellow, thin blades and weak roots	Excessive water
Small bleached spots or circles	Dollar Spot
Dead patches don't green up in the spring on bermuda	Spring Dead Spot

Common Turfgrass Pests

Scenario 2 – Grass affected in irregular patterns:

Symptoms	Possible Causes
Slow decline, yellowish area, restricted shallow roots, wilt	Nematodes
Slow decline, yellowish areas, grass thins out, stunted leaf blades, white cottony mass attached to nodes	Bermuda Mites
Gray cast to foliage, then yellowish brown, leaves become slimy and mat together	Pythium
Yellowish spots with fuzzy orange lesions	Rust
Area fades in color or dries rapidly after watering	Soil variation or septic tank
Grass thin, area wilts quickly, fertilizer doesn't seem to help	Competing tree roots
Tips of leaves bleached, then burned	Salt burn
Weak, elongated growth, thinning lawn	Too much shade
Decay of roots and crown area of grass	Fusarium
Gradual decline of centipede lawn	Centipede Decline
White mildew-like growth on foliage	Powdery Mildew
Distinct lesions on foliage turning yellow	Helminth Leaf Spot
Yellowish or dead spots, grass easily pulled out by roots	Billbugs
Grass blades cut and webbing near surface	Sod Webworms
Damaged roots, dead areas, pearl-like insect in soil	Ground Pearl

Scenario 3 – Grass affected in streaked patterns:

Symptoms	Possible Causes
Grass bleached, yellow, brown, or dead	Chemical burn

Scenario 4 – Grass affected but no particular pattern:

Symptoms	Possible Causes
Yellowish foliage especially on new growth or yellow between veins	Iron deficiency or high pH
Grass blades covered with gray, chalky, powdery growth	Slime Mold
Grass yellowish green on older leaves, eventually brown tips	Nitrogen deficiency
Grass has grayish cast, tips of leaves split or frayed	Dull mower blade
Grass spongy, runners exposed on surface	Thatch
Weeds present	Compaction, poor management

Grass thin, weak, and just doesn't respond despite everything done right	Variety not adapted to area
Stems and leaves turn reddish-purple color	Cold temperature reaction
Mottled yellowish-brown appearance in fall or early spring	Frost damage
Grayish lesions with purplish margins on stems and leaves	Gray Leaf Spot
Linear, grayish-white streaks on leaf blades	Downy Mildew
Yellow mottled leaf blades, overall stunted appearance	St. Augustine Decline Virus
Large ant mounds	Fire Ants
Frothy, spit-like substance on grass	Spittlebugs
Cottony substance on grass stems	Mealybugs
Soil hard and scum, mold, or algae present	Soil compaction, poor drainage, too much shade
Roots cut off, dead areas in lawn, pulls up easily	White Grubs
Stems chewed near soil surface, wilting and dead	Cutworms
Grass bleached or speckled, hopping insects	Leafhoppers

Weeds

You've probably heard this before, but a weed is any plant out of place. A high percentage of lawn weeds are annuals that need sunlight to germinate. Thinning lawns are an invitation for sunlight to penetrate the soil, allowing the weed seed to germinate, and so the battle begins. Some of our prized turf species even act as weeds. And because these warm-season lawn grasses can be so aggressive, just having a thick, healthy lawn will keep most sun-loving weeds out.

Learn to distinguish a grassy weed from a broad-leaf weed. Then there are the sedges that have minds, and unique roots, of their own.

Grassy weeds are called monocots, meaning that a single seed leaf (cotyledon) emerges from the seed. Grasses typically have leaf blades with veins that run parallel to each other. The most common example is crabgrass.

Broadleaf weeds, on the other hand, are dicots, meaning that two leaves emerge from the seed. The veins of broadleaf weeds typically form a net-like pattern on the leaf. The most infamous is dandelion.

Nutsedges differ because they are not really a grass or a broadleaf weed—they are lawn "aliens," if you will. They have triangular stems that don't easily pull out of the ground. The roots go deep, with many species having little nut-lets attached (thus the name), which, if broken off during weeding, quickly form their own new plants. There are many different species of nutsedge that can invade lawns.

Grassy, broadleaf, or nutsedge weeds can either be annual, perennial, or biennial. Annuals live one year and reseed for the following year's growth. Perennials live more than one year, typically going through a dormant period, then reemerging the next season from an underground stem or crown. In their first year, biennials grow only foliage and may or may not go dormant. The second year, the plant sends up flowers, then sets seed before it dies.

These simple classifications are important in knowing how to manage weed infestations. For example, weeds such as crabgrass that germinate from seed can be restrained either before the seeds germinate, which is called "pre-emergent" control, or after the plants are up and growing, which is called "post-emergent" control.

Knowing if a particular weed's optimum growing time is the warm or cool season also helps. Winter annuals, such as henbit, germinate in the fall. So pre-emergent control would need to be applied in late summer or early fall before the weed seeds germinate.

The following list of weeds is not all inclusive, but it does contain some of the most common lawn weeds. They are shown by category to help with iden-tification and times of control.

Winter Grassy Weeds

Use pre-emergent control in late summer or early fall depending on mois-ture and temperature; use post-emergent control any time after weeds are up and growing, following guidelines on product label.

Annual Bluegrass

Winter Broadleaf Weeds

Use pre-emergent control in late summer or fall depending on moisture and temperature; use post-emergent control any time after weeds are up and growing, following guidelines on product label.

Henbit   *Purple Deadnettle*

Common Chickweed   *Hairy Bittercress*

Dandelion (perennial)   *White Clover (perennial)*

Summer Broadleaf Weeds

Use pre-emergent control in early to late spring depending on temperature and moisture; use post-emergent control any time after weeds are up and growing, following guidelines on product label.

Spotted Spurge

Lawn Burweed

Dichondra (perennial)

Summer Grassy Weeds

Use pre-emergent control in early to late spring depending on temperature and moisture; use post-emergent control any time after weeds are up and growing, following guidelines on product label.

Crabgrass

Goosegrass

Southern Sandbur

Field Sandbur

Dallisgrass (perennial)

Sedges

Most products are for post-emergent management.

Annual Sedge

Yellow Nutsedge

Purple Nutsedge

As a general rule, grassy weeds can be grouped together when selecting herbicides for control. The same holds true for broadleaf weeds and sedges. If you have difficulty identifying a weed, contact a university, botanical garden, or extension agent. Most importantly, read the product label to see what specific weeds are listed for control, and apply the herbicide at the appropriate time. Don't forget to make sure the product is labeled for safe use with your particular type of lawn. Always, always read the label before you purchase a product, before you apply it, and before you store or dispose of it. Any herbicide application can affect your newly planted or overseeded lawn, flower beds, trees, vegetable garden, pets, children, and even neighbors if you are not careful.

I've chosen not to list specific herbicides because they vary from region to region and are on and off the market from one year to the next. Plus, new products are introduced on a regular basis. Just remember to match the product label to the weed you are trying to control, whether it is grass, broadleaf, or sedge, and to the season in which you plan to apply the herbicide.

There are also natural or organic products to consider. As a matter of fact, the harsher chemicals should be used as a last resort, and even then only if you have reasonable expectations about your lawn's appearance.

Natural or Organic Herbicides

Watch for specially formulated products on the market made of vinegar and lemon juice, herbicidal soap, fatty acids, and even cornmeal (maize gluten meal). The cornmeal products have been receiving a lot of attention and can work as a pre-emergent or post-emergent control depending on the brand. Follow the same principles as with non-organic herbicides in terms of reading the label and matching the product to the weed and type of lawn grass. Creating and mixing your own formulation is risky. Labeled products have been tested extensively in terms of rate of application and appropriate use. Just because a product is "organic" doesn't mean you can take shortcuts with safety. Read the label. Follow directions. More is not better. Wear gloves and other protective clothing as recommended.

Insects

Insects definitely can be described as "the good, the bad, and the ugly." Unfortunately, many folks categorize all insects as bad, pulling out the chemicals at the first sign of movement. There truly are good insects that feed on bad insects in the lawn. Therefore, learning to identify insects can be very helpful in knowing if you need to do anything to them, and, if so, what and how.

Some types of lawn grass have been bred to resist feeding insects. For example, some cultivars of cool-season turf, such as fescue, contain fungi known as endophytes that repel or kill certain pests, including sod webworms, armyworms, billbugs, parasitic nematodes, and chinch bugs. Many seed labels don't say whether the particular cultivar contains endophytes or not, and asking the retailer to check with the distributor may be the only way to find out.

Preventive spraying should never be done. The first step is to identify, and if at all possible, count, the insects so you can devise a management solution. I like to call it "scout and count." Be active in your landscape, scouting for signs, symptoms, and the pests themselves. Then count the number present within a given area, such as one square foot. This practice is a part of Integrated Pest Management, a system that tries to work with nature to control damaging insects. With many insect pests, there are predetermined threshold numbers that indicate whether any action should be taken. These numbers are just guidelines. Environmental factors, foot traffic, soil type, specific grass cultivar, and overall management practices dictate how much a lawn can tolerate before serious symptoms appear and the lawn is in danger. In most cases, lawns are quite resilient.

One of the best ways to scout for foliage-feeding insects is to make a drench of water and dishwashing detergent. Mix 2-4 tablespoons of dishwashing detergent to 1-2 gallons of water. With concentrated detergents, use $1^1/_2$ tablespoons per gallon. Pour the mix over a square foot area where you have noted symptoms. Or cut a hole in a coffee can, push the can into the affected site, and pour the mix into the can so the solution will be forced further down into the soil. Wait and watch for about ten minutes for any critters that might work their way into the solution or float to the surface. This practice doesn't work well with soil- or root-feeding insects such as cutworms or grubs. These are best found by cutting into the sod at least 3-4 inches deep on three sides. Then lift up the piece of sod by using a trowel or shovel in a technique similar to lifting a brownie from a cake pan with a spatula.

Once the insects have been identified, remember that a few bad guys here and there may not be worth any action at all. Some insects do not cause damage in small numbers. And a healthy lawn will almost always outgrow any minimal insect damage. But several bad guys in a small area may be a different story depending on what they are and the kind of damage they can cause.

If an insecticide is deemed necessary, you must read the label to see how it works. Is it a contact spray requiring direct application to the insect, or is it a systemic that can be sprayed on foliage or roots to discourage the pest? Systemic insecticides are seldom effective in preventing pests over the long term. Most insecticides are intended for direct contact applications or as occasional short-term deterrents.

Insects are also cyclical. They complete their life cycle (one generation) with various stages of growth at various times of year. Some overwinter, others migrate. Most insects cause damage only at certain stages of their life cycle, and even when at that stage may be a problem only for a few weeks. Others may be damaging for the entire growing season. These are factors you must study in order to manage the situation without harming your family, pets, environment, and beneficial insects.

You would be surprised at how many good or beneficial insects inhabit our lawns. Some of them have voracious appetites that keep many of the bad guys under control. Planting legumes or nectar plants in a flower bed or garden adjoining the lawn can help bring the good guys into your landscape to work on your lawn. But if you use harsh chemicals, even some organic ones, on a regular basis, you very well may be eliminating the insects that nature intended to do the work for you.

Organic Insecticides

It is imperative that you read the label when shopping for organic insecticides for the lawn. For example, "Bt" or *Bacillus thuringiensis* is known to control caterpillar larvae, but doesn't control every kind of moth or butterfly larvae, only certain ones. There are also specific varieties of Bt on the market. Some don't work on larvae at all. And some types of Bt can harm butterfly larvae you may be trying to attract to the landscape. Reading the label is the only way to know a given product will work for sod webworms, armyworms, or both. Some organic products may not be labeled for lawn grass at all. Some to consider are Neem, pyrethrin, canola oil, vegetable oil, diatomaceous earth, rotenone, Bt, *Beauveria bassiana,* and horticultural oils. These products are sold in various forms, mixes, and brands.

Beneficial Insects

Beneficial Insect	Feeds On
Ant Lion (Doodlebug)	Caterpillars, aphids, and many other soil insects
Assassin Bug (Wheel Bug)	Assortment of insects, but can bite you also
Big-eyed Bug	Chinch bugs, assorted insect eggs, small larvae, and soft-bodied insects
Damsel Bug	Aphids, assorted insect eggs, small larvae, and many other soft-bodied insects
Earthworm*	Doesn't feed on insects but good for the soil, although too many can make the soil level lumpy. Verti-cutting the soil can help with this rare problem.
Earwig	Can also feed on plants, but is typically a predator and eats chinch bugs, webworms, and other soil insects
Green Lacewing (Aphid Lion)	Small caterpillars, aphids, mites, thrips, mealybugs, soft bodied insects, and insect eggs
Ground Beetle	Feeds on almost any soil insect, particularly cutworms, armyworms, sod webworms, and small mole crickets
Ladybug Beetle (Ladybird Beetle)	Adults and larvae feed on small, soft-bodied insects such as aphids, mites, scale, and insect eggs

Beneficial Insects (cont.)

Beneficial Insect	Feeds On
Minute Pirate Bug	Thrips, spider mites, and assorted insect eggs
Nematode	Beneficial nematodes (*Steinernema* and *Heterohabditis* species) can feed on assorted caterpillar larvae or grubs, and flea larvae
Predaceous Stinkbug	Feeds on many assorted insects including caterpillar larvae
Praying Mantis	Feeds on almost any other insect. including other beneficials
Rove Beetle	Aphids, nematodes, most soil inhabiting larvae
Spined Soldier Bug	Fall armyworm and other caterpillar larvae
Spider*	Feeds on an assortment of pests, including beetles, caterpillars, leafhoppers, and aphids
Syrphid Fly (Hover Fly)	Larval stage feeds on soft-bodied insects such as aphids
Parasitic Wasp	Crickets, caterpillars, and aphids

*not technically insects, but beneficial nonetheless

Learn to recognize good bugs in all their stages—a ladybug beetle larva doesn't look at all like a ladybug.

Most Wanted List *(but not in your lawn)*

There are some pests, such as aphids, grasshoppers, whiteflies, and spider mites, that are likely to be found on pretty much any kind of plant. The following insects are more common in certain species of turf.

Armyworm

Pseudaletia unipuncta and related species

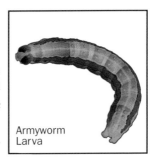

Armyworm Larva

Favored Hosts: Bermuda, Carpet, St. Augustine, Zoysia, Kentucky Bluegrass, and Tall Fescue. All lawn grasses are potentially at risk during severe outbreaks.

Feeding Time: Spring (April-June) and Fall (July-November), typically feed during the day.

Overwinter As: Usually as larvae, sometimes further south, and migrate north as adult moths.

Detrimental Stage: Larvae in soil, thatch, and debris.

Life Cycle: Dormant larvae resume surface feeding in the spring, eventually returning to the soil to pupate, changing to flying adult moths that lay eggs to start the cycle all over again. There can be as many as five generations per year depending on the location and climate.

Armyworm Adult

Insect Description: Large, pale green caterpillars up to 1¹/₂ inches long when fully grown with distinct yellow to brownish-green stripes. When disturbed, the caterpillars may curl into a "c" shape. The adult moths are a dull pale brown to gray color with a white spot in the center of each forewing. They can have wingspans of 1¹/₄-1¹/₂ inches wide. The eggs are greenish white and spherical, laid in masses. The pupae are initially reddish brown, but turn almost black before they change into adults. Color varies among species.

Damage Symptoms and Signs: Individual leaf blades, as well as the root crowns, are chewed and eaten. With severe infestations, the lawn can develop circular bare spots.

Scout and Count: Severe damage can occur if there are more than five per square yard. The soap-flush mixture can help force them to the surface for identification during the day.

Management: Just because there are adults present doesn't mean there will be a bad outbreak of larvae. Natural predators, parasites, disease, and environmental conditions can deter the actual larval numbers. Be observant and watch for the larvae presence and symptoms of feeding. Contact sprays labeled for armyworm or caterpillars are best applied when large numbers and extensive damage dictate control.

Bermuda Mite

(Eriophyid Mite)
Eriophyes cynodoiensis

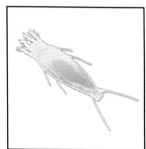

Favored Hosts: Bermuda.

Feeding Time: Any time during growing season.

Overwinter As: Adults and eggs in thatch and beneath leaf sheaths.

Detrimental Stage: Adults suck plant juices from stems and inside leaf sheaths.

Life Cycle: The adults lay eggs that hatch into nymphs in about five to seven days, then grow into adults. It doesn't take long for high populations to build up. The species is most active in late spring and summer.

Insect Description: Microscopic in size, creamy white, worm-like mites with two pairs of legs near head. Not the same as a spider mite. Eggs are oval and transparent to opaque. The nymphs are two-thirds the size of the adults, which are about $1/125$ inch long and whitish in color.

Damage Symptoms and Signs: Individual plants become stunted or tufted. The stems or internodes become shortened. Highly infested grass can thin, turn brown, and die. Areas adjoining fence rows or property lines are most at risk. Symptoms typically occur in the summer and fall.

Scout and Count: They are hard to count, and thresholds are not typically given. First look for the symptoms, and then tap the grass onto a white sheet of paper. Watch to see if any dust specks on the paper start to crawl. A hand lens or microscope can also help magnify the tiny adults for a better look, or take the stunted grass to a professional for assistance in identification.

Management: Apply controls when mites and symptoms are present. Miticides or oil-based insecticides work best and should be labeled specifically for mites and lawn grass. Mixing these pesticides with a wetting agent or surfactant to make them adhere to the grass and insects is helpful. Collect grass clippings and dispose of them properly. Mow at closest recommended setting without scalping the lawn.

Billbug

(Hunting, Zoysia, or Bluegrass Billbug)

Sphenophorus species

Billbug
Larva

Favored Hosts: Bermuda, Centipede, Kentucky Bluegrass, and Zoysia.

Feeding Time: Spring through fall.

Overwinter As: Adults hibernating in grass, in warmer climates larvae and pupae can also over-winter.

Detrimental Stage: Adults and larvae.

Life Cycle: Adults emerge in spring, feeding on leaves and burrowing into stems where they lay eggs. Larvae hatch and feed on grass stems and roots during the growing season before they change into adults in the fall. There is typically one generation per year.

Billbug
Adult

Insect Description: Adults are typically around ³/₈ inch long, black or brown beetles with a snout typical of a weevil. There can be more than one species present. The larvae are also about ³/₈ inch long, resembling white grubs but not as big, legless, white in color with a yellowish or brownish head. The creamy white eggs are elongated and turn yellow before hatching. The pupa is a pale yellow, almost white, similar to the adult in shape.

Damage Symptoms and Signs: Most signs show up in late summer when the grass is usually under stress from heat and drought. Small areas turn yellow, then brown, and the grass can eventually die. In these areas, the grass can be pulled out by hand and easily lifted from the soil where the chewing has occurred. A sawdust-like material known as frass is usually present on the stem where the chewing has taken place.

Scout and Count: Cut sod in border of damaged area and remove. The threshold of tolerance is three to five grubs or ten adults per square foot.

Management: Just because adults are seen does not mean treatment is necessary. Oftentimes, they do not cause obvious damage. Treatment should be considered when symptoms are seen, insects have been identified, and populations counted to see if the numbers are near the threshold amount. Then appropriately labeled insecticides can be applied as a drench according to directions, usually in May, June, or July to control the grubs.

Chinch Bug

(Southern Chinch Bug)

Blissu insularis

Favored Hosts: Primarily St. Augustine, but occasionally Centipede and Bermuda in Gulf States.

Feeding Time: Hot dry weather during the summer.

Overwinter As: Mainly as eggs, sometimes as adults in leaf nodes, blades, thatch, or debris, but can remain active in any stage through the winter in southernmost locales or in very warm, dry winters.

Detrimental Stage: Primarily nymphs but adults as well can extract plant juices with needle-like mouthparts.

Life Cycle: Overwintering eggs hatch into nymphs that infest lawns. Nymphs about $^1/_{20}$ inch long develop into adults about $^1/_5$ inch in two to six weeks depending on environmental conditions. There can be three to five generations per year with higher populations in the summer.

Insect Description: Adults are black with white patches on the wings. Each wing has a distinctive triangular black mark. The pale yellow eggs, which turn red before hatching, are flattened at one end with three to five distinct minute projections. The nymphs resemble the adults but are wingless and smaller. The head and thorax are brown and the eyes are red. The abdomen is pale yellow or light red with a black top.

Damage Symptoms and Signs: The feeding occurs primarily on the tender basal leaves and feeding areas in the grass begin to yellow, soon becoming brown, circular dead spots. As the grass dies the nymphs move to the periphery of the dead areas, causing the spots to enlarge.

Scout and Count: The adults and nymphs are typically concentrated near the soil surface. They can be easily flushed to the surface for identification with a soapy water drench in the damaged areas. Usually twenty to twenty-five nymphs or adults per square foot, along with initial symptoms, means a management practice should be implemented.

Management: Chinch bugs are naturally attacked by fungal disease as well as beneficial insects and can often be kept at bay. A few adults or nymphs does not always dictate a response in chemicals. Healthy lawns, properly watered with deep and infrequent irrigation, are most resistant to the pest. Symptoms and insect populations in the threshold range signify a probable concern that may require some action. Soil drenches as a contact application are best and should be labeled for chinch bug control. Watering the lawn before application is also of great benefit. When renovating or putting in a new lawn, look for chinch bug resistant cultivars such as 'Floratam'. Reduce nitrogen rates and use slow release fertilizers. Control thatch, and mow at highest recommended setting with sharp blades.

Cutworm

Several species

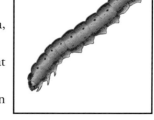

Favored Hosts: Most turfgrasses but favors Bermuda, Carpet, Zoysia, Kentucky Bluegrass, and Fescue.
Feeding Time: Growing season and feeds primarily at night or on cloudy days.
Overwinter As: Pupae or mature, inactive larvae in soil.
Detrimental Stage: Larvae severing plant stems and roots.
Life Cycle: In the spring, the overwintering forms turn into adults that feed at night. The females lay numerous eggs in clusters hatching in three to five days. The larvae go through several stages before pupating into adults. As many as four generations can occur per year.
Insect Description: Adult moths are dark brown with patterned forewings and lightly brown hindwings. The eggs are white and round, becoming somewhat darker prior to hatching. The fat larvae can reach $1^1/2$ inches in length or more. They can be brown, gray, or black and are usually quite dull in color depending on the species. They characteristically curl into a "c" shape when disturbed. The pupa is brown.
Damage Symptoms and Signs: Stems are chewed near the soil surface. The areas wilt, eventually turning brown and becoming spotty in appearance.
Scout and Count: The threshold range is six to sixteen per square foot.
Management: Control seldom is needed unless symptoms are evident, and larvae numbers are within the threshold range. Insecticide soil drenches work best in the impacted areas. I've even heard of scattering self-rising flour in the problem area just before dark. Supposedly they favor the flour, and when it rises—well, you get the point.

Fire Ant

Several species but imported red fire ant,
Solenopsis invicta, is most troublesome

Favored Hosts: Typically they don't harm grass, just make unsightly mounds. Instead, they are more of a nuisance to homeowners and pets. Feed on insects, plant seeds, and are predators to some lawn pests.

Feeding Time: All season.

Overwinter As: All stages.

Detrimental Stage: Each ant is capable of biting and stinging several times.

Life Cycle: The colony is made up of winged fertile females, known as queens, which lay eggs; winged males; and assorted sizes of worker ants. The males die shortly after mating with the queens. The workers perform various tasks to keep the colony running.

Insect Description: All ant species look similar to the imported red fire ant, so positive identification is tricky. Relying on entomologists for positive species identification sometimes is best. Mounds are the most characteristic means of identification and are typically larger than those built by most ants.

Damage Symptoms and Signs: Large, unsightly mounds in lawn. More likely in drier soils. Painful stings and bites.

Scout and Count: One mound is too many.

Management: Since the ants are scavengers, applying recommended granules or baits is the easiest and oftentimes the best practice. Drenches also can work, but it is hard to penetrate the entire colony before large numbers escape. Biological controls are available as well, but they may take longer to kill the colony. Do not disturb the colony first, or the ants will scatter. Other recommendations are to treat the entire lawn with bait between late August and mid-October, and then treat individual problem mounds with a drench, granule, bait, or dust as needed.

Ground Pearl

(Soil or Ground Mealybugs)
Margarodes spp.

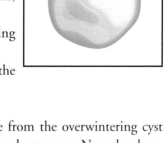

Favored Hosts: Bermuda, Centipede, St. Augustine, and Zoysia.

Feeding Time: Late spring throughout growing season.

Overwinter As: Nymphs or as cysts, also known as the "ground pearl" stage.

Detrimental Stage: Nymph.

Life Cycle: Adult females about $^1/_{16}$ inch emerge from the overwintering cyst stage, then deposit eggs in the soil throughout early summer. Nymphs about the size of a grain of sand emerge in mid-summer, infesting grass roots and rhizomes. Once the nymphs attach and begin feeding by extracting plant juices, they develop the familiar, round, pearl-like appearance and increase in size. Typically there is one generation per year but they can remain in the ground pearl stage for years depending on environmental conditions.

Insect Description: The adult female is basically a pinkish scale insect with small forelegs and claws. The male is gnatlike. The egg clusters are pinkish white and enclosed in a white waxy sac. The nymph is slender at first, later forming a hard, globular, encysted, dingy yellow to purple shell known as a ground pearl.

Damage Symptoms and Signs: Symptoms are most apparent during drought when the damaged grass roots undergo stress. The lawn develops irregular patches of yellow, sometimes wilted, grass that can eventually turn brown and die.

Scout and Count: There are no threshold guidelines to date.

Management: Insecticides have not proven very effective. A healthy, well-managed lawn, especially one properly watered during drought situations, is the key to prevention.

Leafhopper

Several species but *Carneocephala*
is quite common

Favored Hosts: Almost any lawn grass.

Feeding Time: Throughout the growing season.

Overwinter As: Eggs or adults in plant debris.

Detrimental Stage: Adults and nymphs.

Life Cycle: Adults begin to feed and mate in the
spring, laying eggs in the leaf blades of the grass. Two weeks later, the eggs
hatch into nymphs that mature and grow into adults. There can be as many
as four generations depending on species and location.

Insect Description: Adult leafhoppers, as the name implies, hop, or they can fly.
They are typically less than $1/5$ inch with a triangular shape and characteristic
folded wings over their bodies. Colors can vary depending on species from
yellow to green to gray. The white eggs are elongated in shape. The nymphs
are the same shape as the adults, just paler in color, smaller, and wingless.

Damage Symptoms and Signs: Leafhoppers have piercing-sucking mouthparts that
extract the plant's sap. Heavy infestations can cause speckled or bleached looking leaf blades that can be confused with drought or disease damage.

Scout and Count: Trying to chase a leafhopper is like trying to catch a grasshopper.
As a result, thresholds have not been developed to date.

Management: Seldom do they cause severe problems on established, well-
managed lawns. Seedlings and sprigs in newly planted lawns are more at risk.
There are insecticides labeled for leafhopper control, but as you can imagine,
it is difficult to spray localized areas, so in many cases the entire lawn needs to
be treated. Repeat applications are often needed with severe outbreaks.

Mealybug

(Mealybug Scale or Grass Scale)
Several species but the Rhodesgrass
Mealybug, *Antonina graminis,* is most
common in the South

Favored Hosts: Almost any grass is at risk, but Bermuda and St. Augustine tend to be favored.

Feeding Time: Any time during growing season.

Overwinter As: Adults but can also overwinter as nymphs in warmer climates in thatch and other lawn debris.

Detrimental Stage: Adults and nymphs.

Life Cycle: The adults give birth to crawling nymphs. There are no eggs. The nymphs attach themselves to grass crowns, stems, nodes, leaf sheaths, or just about anything with some protection. Unlike their relative ground pearl scale, they feed on aboveground parts. Mealybugs insert their mouthparts into the plant and feed on the plant juices. After feeding begins, they form a white protective covering that is waxy and cottony, and is a distinctive characteristic of mealybugs. With time, the nymphs grow into adults, ranging in size from $^1/_{25}$-$^1/_8$ inch. There can be as many as five generations per year.

Insect Description: The purplish-brown adults are almost glob-like in appearance with no legs. The oval body is enclosed by a white, waxy sac that turns yellow with age. The nymphs look like the adults, only smaller, and with legs so they can crawl. They change size before maturing into non-mobile adults.

Damage Symptoms and Signs: Heavy infestations can harm grass in small irregular areas, initially turning yellow then brown. Individual blades first become discolored with the cotton-like pest. Localized infestations can resemble fertilizer caked around the grass stems.

Scout and Count: No threshold ranges have been determined to date.

Management: Watch for insects and any symptoms. Collect grass clippings and destroy or properly compost with intensive heat. Spray if damage to the leaf blades appears and begins to spread. Use appropriately labeled insecticides.

Mole Cricket

Several species with *Scapteriscus* being the most damaging

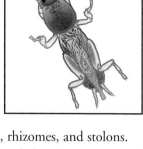

Favored Hosts: Bermuda, Carpet, Centipede, and St. Augustine.

Feeding Time: Growing season in coastal areas, spring and summer for cooler areas.

Overwinter As: Nymphs in soil.

Detrimental Stage: Adults or nymphs feeding on roots, rhizomes, and stolons.

Life Cycle: Nymphs become active in spring, feeding and changing in size until they become mature adults in early summer. The adults have wings and can fly during the mating period. Eggs are laid in the soil and hatch ten to forty days later, depending on temperatures, into immature, small, wingless nymphs. There is typically one generation per year.

Insect Description: The adults resemble a cross between a cricket and a mole, maturing to about $1^1/2$ inches long. They are brown with fine hairs giving them a velvety look. They have a snout, and mole-like front legs for digging. The greenish eggs are oval. The nymphs look just like the adults except wingless and smaller.

Damage Symptoms and Signs: The grass roots and stems are impacted by severe feeding due to high populations, which causes the grass to turn yellow, brown, and die, typically in a circular pattern. The nymphs move out to the edges of the grass as it dies. The tunneling and burrowing habits can also disturb plant roots, especially during the establishment of new lawns. Areas near light poles and in full sun are more likely to attract the adults during mating. Most of the feeding occurs at night.

Scout and Count: Two or three per square foot. Soap mixes can help flush them to the surface.

Management: As with all insect pests, chemical control should be a last resort, used only when visible damage and high numbers indicate a problem. Liquid contact insecticides labeled for mole crickets can be applied as a drench, and granular types can be broadcast and lightly watered into the affected areas. The best results are in June or early July when the nymphs are small. Bait also works, especially in the fall when the nymphs are trying to store up reserves for their winter rest, but do not water for several days after applying bait. Good management practices are the best defense.

Sod Webworm

Several species with *Crambus* and *Parapediasia* being the most prominent

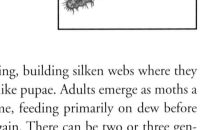

Favored Hosts: Almost any turfgrass, especially Bermuda, Carpet, Centipede, Kentucky Bluegrass, St. Augustine, and Zoysia.

Feeding Time: Spring through summer.

Overwinter As: Larvae below soil line.

Detrimental Stage: Larvae.

Life Cycle: Larvae start feeding in early spring, building silken webs where they feed, and developing into silken cocoon-like pupae. Adults emerge as moths a few weeks later and only live a short time, feeding primarily on dew before they lay eggs to start the cycle all over again. There can be two or three generations per year depending on species and environmental conditions. They are typically night feeders during the heat of the summer.

Insect Description: The moths vary among species but are typically a dull grayish-brown with streaks at the base of the front wings. They fold their wings like a tent when resting and are very weak flyers. They are active primarily at dusk, near the soil surface. Eggs are tiny, oblong, and white to pale yellow in color. The larvae can reach up to $3/4$ inch in length. They vary among species but typically are pinkish white to yellowish brown with coarse hairs and spots on each segment. Pupa is reddish-brown.

Damage Symptoms and Signs: The larvae cut the grass blades off just above the soil or thatch line, and pull the blades into their feeding tunnels at the soil surface. Severe infestations are indicated by grass cropped in irregular patterns that can also turn brown. Hot, dry weather is when the symptoms are most obvious. Web-like material is usually present near the soil or thatch line on closer inspection.

Scout and Count: Six to twelve webworms per square foot. A soap and water mix drenched onto the damaged area can force the webworms to the surface for identification and counting purposes. Or take a flashlight out at night, and pull the grass apart to look for feeding larvae and web-like material.

Management: If symptoms and high infestation warrant, contact insecticides labeled for sod webworms can be applied as a spray or drench and lightly watered into the grass.

White Grubs

Japanese Beetle Larvae, *Popillia japonica*, May or June Beetle or June Bug Larvae, *Phyllophaga* spp.

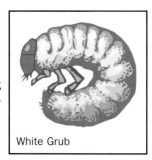

White Grub

Favored Hosts: Almost any lawn grass including Bermuda, Carpet, Centipede, Fescue, Kentucky Bluegrass, and Zoysia.

Feeding Time: Any time during the growing season. Japanese beetles are more prevalent in northern locales such as North Carolina and Tennessee and aren't as likely to be found in the coastal or plains areas to date. May beetles, on the other hand, are prevalent in most states.

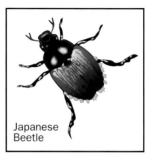

Japanese Beetle

Overwinter As: Larvae (or grubs) for Japanese beetle, larvae and adults for May beetle.

Detrimental Stage: Larvae feeding on grass roots and rhizomes.

Life Cycle: Larvae become active in spring, feeding on grass roots 1-3 inches deep for several days until they pupate. Adults emerge in late spring or summer, later laying eggs that hatch into larvae in the fall. There is typically one generation per year.

May Beetle

Insect Description: Japanese beetle adults are oval in shape, about $7/16$ to $1/2$ inch long, with a shiny green body. White hairs occur on the abdomen behind the wings. Patches of white are also located on each side of the body. May or June beetle adults are slightly bigger, reaching up to $3/4$ inch. They are a shiny, reddish-brown to almost black color, with an oblong body shape. The eggs are pearly white and oblong. Larvae resemble Japanese beetles in shape but are whiter in color with a distinct brown head. Both larvae can range in size from $1/4$-$1\,1/4$ inches. June beetle pupae are dull brown.

Damage Symptoms and Signs: The roots are severed and eaten. As a result, large areas of yellowing grass begins to die, eventually turning brown in an irregular mosaic pattern. Initially can look like localized drought stress. When the grass is lifted by mower blades, it easily releases from the ground because of the severed roots. The lawn can also feel spongy when you walk across impacted areas.

Scout and Count: Pull or cut up the sod in damaged areas to count the number of grubs. Six to ten per square foot generally warrants possible treatment.

Management: Commercial products of organic milky spore disease are effective in managing the Japanese beetles only. The bacterial spores kill the grubs when applied according to directions in late summer up until fall. It has no effect on May or June beetles. Insecticide soil drenches can also be applied and will work on both beetle species but may need to be repeated during the season. Raising the mowing height and using a sharp blade will help avoid further stress to the grass. *Bacillus thuringiensis* 'Japonensis' is an organic product being tested with promising results for May or June beetle grub control, and it may be on the market soon.

Turfgrass Diseases

Diseases are caused by pathogens, referred to as causal agents or organisms, that feed on or disturb plant tissue. They are typically fungal or bacterial in nature and spread by rain, wind, and, in some cases, contact with lawn mower tires. For a disease to become infectious, there must be a host (turfgrass), pathogen, and the right environmental conditions such as temperature or moisture. And those conditions must occur for the right amount of time for the pathogen to grow and become infectious. This means that some diseases are more prominent during certain times of the year.

Just as with insects, homeowners must be observant of their lawns to spot symptoms early. Diseases sometimes spread very quickly, and early identification is the key to implementing the appropriate management strategy. Some diseases can be managed by changing cultural habits, such as fertilizer applications, watering, and mowing. If chemical treatments are required, early detection can help in treating only the infected area rather than the entire lawn. This saves time and money and helps protect the environment from an overuse of chemicals.

If you do not make a habit of routinely scouting your lawn, it is likely that by the time you see the symptoms of the disease, the pathogen may no longer be active. In other words, the damage is already done, and any kind of control may be a waste of time. If so, it may be time for a little lawn renovation. On the other hand, some diseases worsen with time, proper environmental conditions, and poor lawn management, even to the point of killing the grass, roots and all.

Proper Identification

Unfortunately, the symptoms of some lawn diseases resemble not only each other, but also insect damage, or even environmental stress. Learning to identify the diseases is essential. Use the questions in the "Process of Elimination" section and the symptom chart earlier in this chapter, along with the descriptions and photos of several common diseases, as a starting point. If you still are unsure about the problem, most state Cooperative Extension Services have diagnostic labs that can help. Collecting the proper samples determines whether you get a proper identification or not. Taking completely brown, dehydrated, dead samples is no good. All the lab can tell you is the grass is dead. Since secondary organisms move in to decompose dead grass, it is impossible to identify the causal agent at that point. Instead, collect samples that are in different stages of decline. Early stages include water-soaked areas, leaf spots, and wilted or yellowing blades. Also take random samples within the infected area, including roots and stems. Avoid putting the samples in plastic bags in a hot sunny car, or they can turn to mush quickly. Most diagnostic labs have guidelines on properly collecting and submitting samples.

Fungicides

There are several fungicides on the market that can help in lawn disease control. Remember that in many cases, simple cultural or management practices can do the job without spraying. In situations where they can't, you must match the chemical product to your particular disease and lawn grass. Fungicides can be used in many ways depending on the formulation. Some are preventive, some systemic, and others kill on contact. I can't emphasize enough that reading the label is essential in applying the treatment correctly and safely.

Alternative Disease-Control Products

There are many alternative disease-control products available. Look for products such as copper, fungicidal soaps, Neem, baking soda, and sulfur, to mention a few. Again, be sure to read the label. Some products, even organic ones, can burn plant foliage when used in the heat of the day or if air temperatures are too high. Be careful with home concoctions, since application amounts and plant sensitivity are hard to determine.

Common Lawn Diseases

Brown Patch

(Rhizoctonia Blight)
Rhizoctonia solani

Grasses at Risk: Bermuda, Carpet, Centipede, Kentucky Bluegrass, Fescue, St. Augustine, and Zoysia.

Season of Occurrence: Spring and summer for warm-season grasses, fall and winter for cool-season grasses.

Environmental Conditions Needed: Warm air conditions over 70° F, prolonged moisture on leaf blades for over eight hours either from rainfall, dew, or late evening irrigation. Most prevalent on grass that is over-watered and receives excessive amounts of nitrogen.

Spread By: Lawn clippings, moisture, and wind.

Symptoms and Signs: Individual leaf blades are affected, starting with small, dull tan lesions, enlarging and turning brown with reddish-brown margins near the soil. The foliage does not melt down with a white slimy appearance as with pythium blight, but the leaf blades do wilt and are easily pulled from the base of the plant. The grass can wilt because water and nutrient uptake are interrupted. The overall appearance of the lawn shows brown spots or patches from a few inches in size up to several feet. The pattern typically has a somewhat circular appearance. The outer limits of the rings are often darker, giving a "smoke ring" look. There usually are unaffected plants within the circles that remain green, producing what is often described as a "frog-eye" or "doughnut" pattern.

Can Resemble: Dog, white grub, and mole cricket damage.

Management: Select a low fertility program avoiding excess nitrogen. Water early in the morning, deeply and infrequently. Mow when grass foliage is completely dry using a sharp blade. Fungicides are recommended and can be applied in the impacted and adjoining areas rather than on the entire lawn. Remove and compost clippings during warm, moist weather to avoid spread. Avoid thatch build-up.

Dollar Spot

Formerly *Sclerotinia homoeo-carpa,* now thought to be a combination of *Moellerodiscus* spp. and *Lanzia* spp.

Grasses at Risk: Bermuda, Centipede, Kentucky Bluegrass, St. Augustine, and Zoysia.

Season of Occurrence: Late spring, summer, and fall.

Environmental Conditions Needed: Stressed lawn from drought and improper soil fertility, mild to cool air temperatures over 70° to 80° F, and extended periods of high humidity and/or cloudy conditions. Mild wet summers. Poor soil fertility.

Spread By: Foot traffic, mower tires, splashing water, or wind.

Symptoms and Signs: Individual leaf blades first turn yellowish-green, progressing to a water-soaked appearance, and finally turning a straw color with reddish-brown margins. This is easier to detect on coarse-bladed grass species. Overall the lawn looks to have distinct, off-color, almost bleached circular patches a few inches in diameter that, in severe cases, can coalesce into patches several feet across. With morning dew, the white fungal growth from the pathogen may be evident on the affected leaf blades.

Can Resemble: Dull lawnmower blade, drought, dog damage, pythium on fine-bladed grasses, and grey leaf spot on coarse-bladed grasses.

Management: Water early in morning, deeply and infrequently. Mow when leaf blades are completely dry. Apply a nitrogen fertilizer at the proper rate. Adopt a routine fertility program. Use appropriately labeled fungicides. Avoid thatch buildup.

Downy Mildew (See photo of powdery mildew which has a similar appearance.)
Sclerophthora macropoda

Grasses at Risk: Fescue, Kentucky Bluegrass, St. Augustine, and Ryegrass.

Season of Occurrence: Spring, early summer, and fall.

Environmental Conditions Needed: Cool, humid, wet conditions with temperatures around 60-70° F. Grass in poorly drained or partially shaded sites is also more vulnerable.

Spread By: Wind, splashing water, and sometimes by mechanical means, such as lawn mower tires.

Symptoms and Signs: Initially white, raised, linear streaks appear parallel to the midvein of the leaf blade. Leaves eventually become yellow and die at the tips. Distortion of the foliage may also occur.

Can Resemble: St. Augustine decline virus.

Management: Avoid watering in the evening. Instead water early or late in the morning. Water deeply and infrequently. Control thatch problems. Fertilizer programs should be reviewed avoiding high nitrogen applications. Fungicides are available and should be labeled appropriately for downy mildew. The pathogen subsides with drier conditions.

Fusarium Blight

Fusarium culmorum

Grasses at Risk: Fescue, Kentucky Bluegrass, and Ryegrass.

Season of Occurrence: Early spring through summer.

Environmental Conditions Needed: Very high humidity and day temperatures around 80-95° F. Grass that is over-fertilized with high rates of nitrogen is more susceptible. Poor soil moisture or drought-stressed plants impeded by thatch are also more at risk.

Spread By: Splashing water, mechanical movement of mower tires, foot traffic, and wind.

Symptoms and Signs: Stunted grass with scattered patches of light green foliage that turns reddish brown, then tan, and finally a straw color. Tufts of green healthy grass will remain in the impacted areas. Fusarium can also affect the roots and crowns of the plants, characterized by brown to reddish decay and pinkish growth of the pathogen during high incidences of rainfall and irrigation.

Can Resemble: Pythium, mole crickets, and brown patch, except brown patch causes individual leaf blade lesions and fusarium does not.

Management: Reduce thatch layer at appropriate time, reduce or eliminate high nitrogen fertilizer applications, water deeply and less often, fungicide products labeled for your particular turfgrass.

Gray Leaf Spot

Piricularia grisea

Grasses at Risk: St. Augustine, Fescue, and Ryegrass.

Season of Occurrence: Spring, late summer, or fall.

Environmental Conditions Needed: Mild temperatures around 75° F and prolonged rainfall. Lawns over-fertilized with high amounts of nitrogen are also susceptible.

Spread By: Moisture, wind, and mechanical means.

Symptoms and Signs: Individual leaf blades get obvious grayish-brownish-red dots, or spots that enlarge to circular or elongated lesions heavily concentrated along the center of the leaf. During optimum wet conditions the spots develop depressed, blue-gray centers with irregular brown margins and a border of yellow-green tissue. With time and severe infection, entire leaf blades can wither and turn brown. In severe cases crowns can be killed as well. Newly established St. Augustine lawns seem to be more susceptible in early spring. Tolerance of the disease increases as the lawn becomes more established.

Can Resemble: Pythium, brown patch, and drought stress.

Management: Reduce nitrogen, water deeply and less often early in the morning, select resistant grass cultivars, use appropriately labeled fungicides, delay over-seeding with ryegrass until later in the season. Avoid soil compaction. Manage any thatch buildup.

Helminthosporium Leaf Spot

(Helminth Leaf Spot)

Formerly *Helminthosporium* spp. now thought to be a combination of *Bipolaris, Curvularia, Drechslera,* and *Exserohilum* species

Grasses at Risk: Bermuda, Kentucky Bluegrass, Fescue, Ryegrass, and Zoysia.

Season of Occurrence: Spring or early summer for warm-season grasses and spring or fall for cool-season lawns.

Environmental Conditions Needed: Warm, wet weather.

Spread By: Wind, water, mowers, and shoes.

Symptoms and Signs: Circular lesions appear as small purplish spots that increase in size, turn brown, then fade to yellow with a brown or darker margin. Some folks even describe the spots as "eye-like." The entire leaf blade can also turn yellow. There are several different species of the pathogen that can have various lesion shapes,

some circular and some in streaks. The older, infected blades can wither and dry, causing a melting effect in the lawn.

Can resemble: Dull mower blade damage or drought stress, except for the distinctive lesions on leaf blades.

Management: One of the easiest diseases to manage by proper maintenance, using recommended mowing height, sharp blade, moderate fertility, supplemental deep and infrequent irrigation, and thatch control. Apply a fertilizer with moderate rate of nitrogen at the time of infection. Allowing the grass to become stressed from drought, then providing irrigation only to let it become stressed again contributes to the problem. In other words, maintain even moisture if possible. Raise mowing height and especially avoid scalping. Remove and compost grass clippings from infested areas. Use appropriately labeled fungicides.

Powdery Mildew

Erysiphe graminis

Grasses at Risk: Bermuda, Fescue, and Kentucky Bluegrass.
Season of Occurrence: Spring and fall.
Environmental Conditions Needed: Reduced air circulation, partial shade, very high humidity, and milder air temperatures.

Spread By: Moisture, wind, and mechanical means, such as foot traffic and mower tires.

Symptoms and Signs: Grayish-white, powdery, mildew-like growths on the leaf blades, which can spread, making areas of the lawn have a grayish-white appearance. Blades can eventually turn yellow.

Can Resemble: Early stages of slime mold and rust, fertilizer burn.

Management: Bag clippings in severe cases and dispose of properly. Avoid watering in the evenings. Use a sharp mower blade. Thin tree branches for more light and air circulation. Use appropriately labeled fungicides according to directions.

Pythium Blight

(Grease Spot, Cottony Blight,
Pythium Root Rot, or Pythium)
Pythium altimum and
P. aphanidermatum

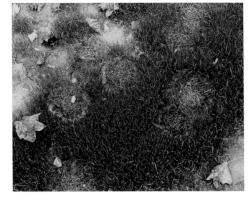

Grasses at Risk: Bermuda, Kentucky Bluegrass, Fescue, and Ryegrass.

Season of Occurrence: Spring and summer for warm-season grasses, fall and winter for cool-season grasses.

Environmental Conditions Needed: Very warm conditions over 85° F, high humidity and extended moisture on leaf blades either from dew, rainfall, or irrigation. Grasses over-fertilized and over-watered are more susceptible as are lawns with poor air circulation in partially shaded sites.

Spread By: Movement of contaminated soil and grass clippings on tires as well as conventional water runoff.

Symptoms and Signs: Individual leaf blades have a water-soaked, grayish-green appearance, shriveling and eventually turning brown. The leaf blades tend to mat together with a slimy look and feel to the foliage. As the disease progresses, irregularly shape areas of turf, usually a few inches across, develop. As it spreads, it encroaches on larger areas. There will also be healthy patches of green in the affected areas, leaving a "frog-eye" appearance. The lawn patches can appear to be irregular, crescent-shaped, or even streaks of blighted grass.

In early morning, with heavy dew or irrigation, cotton-like growth may be seen on the foliage. This same pathogen can also attack roots and is known as pythium root rot. It is commonly present in the soil, and young, emerging seedlings are especially susceptible.

Can Resemble: Dollar spot or dog damage.

Management: Provide good drainage and air circulation. Irrigate early in the morning and avoid frequent irrigation. When the disease is present, avoid foot and mower traffic in the affected area. Labeled fungicides are also available.

Rust

Puccinia spp. and or *Uromyces* spp.

Grasses at Risk: Bermuda, Fescue, Kentucky Bluegrass, Ryegrass, and Zoysia.

Season of Occurrence: Late summer, early fall, or during mild winters for cool-season grasses.

Environmental Conditions Needed: Prolonged periods of cloudy, overcast skies, mild temperatures, and high humidity, followed by sunny weather. Poorly managed lawns with minimal fertilizations, particularly nitrogen-deficient lawns.

Spread By: Primarily by wind and occasionally by splashing water.

Symptoms and Signs: Yellow flecks on leaves that enlarge and become a fuzzy orange-red. The pustules tend to be oriented in rows up and down the leaf blade. If the disease progresses, the leaves turn completely yellow, starting at the tips and moving down toward the sheath. In such cases, the entire area of affected grass appears yellow.

Can Resemble: The early stages of powdery mildew and slime mold. Early stages also resemble fertilizer burn on wet leaf blades.

Management: Fertilize with a slow-release nitrogen product. Remove and compost clippings properly. Mow frequently. Choose resistant cultivars when available. Use appropriately labeled fungicides.

Other Problems

Some lawn problems aren't pathogenic or caused by insects, although the symptoms may look very similar. These problems are often a result of stress, environmental conditions, location, management style, or related to the particular grass selected. Some of the most common are covered in this section.

Bermuda Invasion

Grasses at Risk: Any grass is at risk for bermuda invasion.

Season of Occurrence: Any time during the growing season.

Environmental Conditions Needed: Usually other grasses are stressed, and bermuda keeps on growing, gradually creeping in. Bermuda is also more aggressive than most Southern lawn grasses.

Spread By: Rhizome (underground stems) and stolons (aboveground stems).

Symptoms and Signs: Encroachment into other lawn grasses.

Can Resemble: Bermuda has a look all its own.

Management: Occasionally, properly managed and healthy St. Augustine lawns can resist bermuda invasion, but most of the time bermuda wins out, especially during the onset of drought. As you probably have discovered, digging or pulling bermuda doesn't work unless you get all the underground parts. Bermuda is best controlled by spot treatments using a non-selective herbicide. The non-selective herbicide glyphosate (Roundup™) works but will also kill your desired grass. These types of herbicides should be used in small, localized areas where you are willing to sacrifice some of your favored grass to get rid of the actively growing bermuda. The grass of choice can then be re-planted after several herbicide applications have killed the bermuda, roots and all. Selective herbicides that control only bermuda without damaging other Southern lawn grasses are a rare find.

Centipede Decline

Not identified as any particular pathogen to date, but has been suggested to be caused by the same pathogen responsible for St. Augustine decline virus.

Grasses at Risk: Centipede.

Season of Occurrence: Spring through summer.

Environmental Conditions Needed: Stress conditions such as soil compaction, poor management, especially mowing too close, over-watering, or over-fertilizing with high nitrogen products. Soil pH greater than 6.5.

Spread By: Not known to date.

Symptoms and Signs: The grass gradually deteriorates after a few years and is replaced by weeds and other grasses. Iron chlorosis or yellowing of the leaf blades is usually evident. In severe cases, the grass greens up in the spring but quickly turns off-color, wilts, and dies. The areas affected may be small but can expand up to several feet in diameter. Upon closer examination, the roots have little growth and development. The stolons tend not to be attached to the soil, and the roots may be discolored, especially in lawns with uneven surfaces.

Can Resemble: Drought stress.

Management: Don't mow too high, usually between 1^1/$_2$-3 inches to maintain around 1-^{1}/$_2$ inches tall. Mow with sharp blades. Avoid over-fertilizing with high nitrogen and phosphorus rates in particular. Ideally no more than 1 pound of actual nitrogen per year per 1,000 square feet, divided among three to four applications. Avoid over-watering, especially shallow, frequent applications. Check soil pH.

Fairy Ring

Several species of mushrooms, and puffball-forming fungi.

Grasses at Risk: All warm- and cool-season lawns.

Season of Occurrence: Primarily early spring or late fall.

Environmental Conditions Needed: Dead or decaying organic matter such as tree roots and cool, wet conditions.

Spread By: Mushroom spores are spread by wind and water runoff, and mycelium growth in the soil.

Symptoms and Signs: The fruiting bodies of fungi, known as mushrooms emerge from the ground in a semi-circle or full circle. The grass usually is green near the circle, with lighter yellow bands of grass adjoining it. The dark green rings may also be present without the fruiting structures. Single or multiple rings can occur in the area. They tend to expand each year. Fairy Ring does not harm most turfgrass; it is more of an inconvenience or an eyesore. The fungi are decomposing organic matter in the soil, although there are rare reports of grass being stunted and killed within the ring. Often the soil is more compacted along the ring area due to high amounts of mycelium growth in the soil. This tends to repel fertilizer and supplemental water.

Can Resemble: Symptomatic only of fairy ring.

Management: Fungicide drenches are not a very effective control. Use a commercial wetting agent or make your own using a solution of water and mild dishwashing soap to improve water and fertilizer penetration. Fertilize with a slow-release fertilizer that contains nitrogen, but avoid high rates of nitrogen in the fall. Remove the mushrooms by hand. Aerate the soil in the affected area. Remove branches, roots, and fragments of lumber during any lawn establishment or renovation process.

Grass Going to Seed too Quickly

Grasses at Risk: Primarily seeded grass varieties.

Season of Occurrence: Summer and fall.

Environmental Conditions Needed: Stress from drought, shorter day-length, or nitrogen deficiency.

Spread By: Not applicable.

Symptoms and signs: The grass leaf blades do not seem to grow normally. Seed heads are quick to emerge and are abundant.

Can Resemble: Grasses such as bahia, carpet, buffalo (male varieties in particular), and common bermuda are notorious for sending up seed heads soon after mowing.

Management: If your grass doesn't typically go to seed so quickly, and it has been a while since you last fertilized, apply a nitrogen fertilizer to stimulate faster foliage growth. Water deeply and mow frequently to stimulate more growth. Some seeded varieties tend to go to seed in the fall due to the change in seasons. Other grasses, such as seeded bermuda cultivars, normally bloom and set seed in mid- to late summer.

Iron Chlorosis

Grasses at Risk: Any Southern lawn grass.

Season of Occurrence: During growing season.

Environmental Conditions Needed: Poor fertility program and soil pH greater than 6.5.

Spread By: Not applicable.

Symptoms and Signs: Grass blades tend to turn a light green to light yellow, especially on new growth. Older leaf blades can be yellow between the veins. No signs of a specific disease. Vigor is very poor overall.

Can Resemble: Some disease problems, particularly pythium, dollar spot, and fusarium in the early stages of infection. Can also be confused with nitrogen deficiency, which is a yellowing of younger, newly emerged growth.

Management: Conduct a soil test, and apply lime according to guidelines. Apply a nitrogen fertilizer at the recommended rate. Water thoroughly after application. Mow at the suggested cutting height using a sharp blade. Adapt a fertilizer management program based on a soil test.

Moles

Favored Grasses: Moles don't feed on grass but will tunnel through any lawn.

Feeding Time: Any time soil insect populations are high and soil moisture content makes it easy to dig.

Overwinter As: Hopefully in my neighbor's yard.

Detrimental Stage: Any time they are digging.

Life Cycle: Who cares as long as they do it somewhere else.

Description: Moles are small, furry mammals that are about $3^1/2$-9 inches in length depending on the species. They are known for their front feet that make shallow tunnels under the soil surface as they seek out their favored foods of earthworms, grubs, and other small, soil-inhabiting insects. Moles are often confused with pocket gophers and voles. Pocket gophers seldom dig shallow tunnels but do excavate a noticeable mound that is typically horseshoe-shaped and often plugged with dirt. Gophers feed on seeds, plant roots, and other vegetation. Poisonous peanuts or baits will help to control pocket gophers, as will wooden ground traps with a hole in the end allowing light to enter. Voles are really underground mice. There are several different species, but a common one is known as meadow mice. They tend to favor plant roots, seeds, and stems. They are small, as moles are, but they do not have mole-like feet. They can be easily trapped with a live trap using an apple as the bait. Rodenticides will control them if they are causing severe damage to your lawn. They usually are not a problem on well-managed lawns.

Damage: Moles seldom feed on plants but can damage a plant's root system as they loosen the soil, occasionally uprooting the plant entirely. Newly planted sprigs or plugs are most susceptible to drying out and dying if their roots are disturbed.

Scout and Count: One mole is too many, and that is typically all it takes to make numerous annoying tunnels.

Management: I've learned to live with moles as best I can by trying to think of them as helpfully feeding on pesky grubs, cutworms, ground pearls, and bill-bug larva. The summer droughts seem to discourage them, unless you provide supplemental irrigation, in which case they will come to your lawn from miles around. The only sure way to manage them is to get rid of the insects they feed on, which is virtually impossible, and likely would be harmful to earthworms, depending on which soil insecticide you used. Even then, they would move to the neighbor's lawn until your insect populations built back up, then return for dinner. Baits made of peanuts are of no use, since moles don't usually feed on seeds or plants. Gases, gum, coffee grounds, and cornmeal are all touted as remedies, but research doesn't show very consistent or promising results. Vibrators don't work, and neither do sonic barriers. I suspect the moles actually enjoy them. Whatever you do, don't try gassing them out, whether using liquid or fumes. The soil is too porous, and it is very dangerous. Flooding has the same results, and all you'll get is an expensive water bill. Caster bean has been shown to work somewhat as a repellent, but again with only short-term results. Some dogs and cats are excellent mole-catchers, if you can only teach them not to dig in your yard at the same time. Now you see why I've chosen to live with moles.

Moss/Algae

Grasses at Risk: Any in poor sites.

Season of Occurrence: Spring and fall are ideal but anytime throughout the year.

Environmental Conditions Needed: Waterlogged, compacted, acidic, poor soils, usually in partial or heavy shade, with high humidity and/or rainfall.

Spread By: Moisture and wind.

Symptoms and Signs: Mosses are small plants with fine carpet-like stems. Some folks try to get mosses to grow in suitable sites where grass won't thrive. Algae are thread-like green plants that form a thin, dense scum over the soil surface. Once dried, it becomes black and crusty. Both are non-parasitic to lawn grasses.

Can Resemble: Occasionally molds, but algae and moss have distinctive characteristics.

Management: Maintain good soil fertility and pH. Lime applications may be needed. Improve drainage and add organic material if possible. Be careful when cultivating around trees since shallow roots can be damaged. In some cases, it may be necessary to choose between the tree and the lawn. Increase air and light penetration through proper pruning of trees. Copper sulfate or copper fungicides may be a short-term fix, but follow the label for proper amounts to apply. Once the conditions are corrected, sod can be replanted if the area is not too shady.

Nematodes

Several species of root-feeding nematodes, also referred to as non-segmented roundworms.

Grasses at Risk: All warm- and cool-season grasses, but Centipede, St. Augustine, Bermuda, and Zoysia may be more susceptible depending on the type of nematode.

Season of Occurrence: Late spring and summer.

Environmental Conditions Needed: Typically poor sandy soils low in organic matter. Symptoms occur when grass is stressed, usually in warm weather during drought.

Spread By: Can move through the soil for short distances but is usually spread by mechanical means, such as shovels, tillers, mower tires, and shoes on bare soil, and by runoff moisture.

Symptoms and Signs: Certain areas or even the overall lawn can appear pale and stunted. Overall growth and vigor of the lawn is affected by the root feeding. The roots are not able to withstand drought, cold, or heat stress. The nematodes overwinter in the egg stage. In the spring, as the soil temperatures warm to near 50° F, the eggs hatch into adults. The adults, which are microscopic in size, aggressively feed on the grass roots, impacting the root depth and density. There will also be an absence of normal, healthy, white feeder roots. The symptoms don't show up until later when the grass is stressed during the summer. Weed infestation starts, particularly with sedges and spurges that are not bothered by nematodes. Positive identification can be obtained by taking soil samples to your Cooperative Extension Service for nematode assay tests. The collection of soil for nematode identification is different than for a soil test. Contact your extension staff for guidelines.

Can Resemble: Inadequate watering, low soil fertility, and some lawn decline scenarios.

Management: The addition of organic matter to the soil is the best management strategy if at all possible, since nematodes favor poor sandy soils and not rich organic soils. In lawns with minor damage, proper mowing, feeding, and watering will also enable the grass to be more resilient if attacked by the pests. Deep watering definitely is a benefit since it encourages deeper roots. Colloidal phosphate ground into fine sand and scattered across the lawn has had some positive results in minimizing the numbers, as has ground crab shells known as chitin. Soil sterilants and nematicides are also available but are not labeled for homeowners to use. They should only be applied by a professional with the appropriate pesticide license. Planting an alternative grass is also possible. You could ignore what your neighbors might think and temporarily convert the infected lawn area to cover crops known to reduce nematode populations, such as French marigolds, pangola grass, hairy indigo, or periwinkles, for a season or two in the hope of replanting grass eventually.

Slime Mold

Physarum cinereum, Mucilago spongiosa, and *Fuligo* spp.

Grasses at Risk: All warm- and cool-season grasses.

Season of Occurrence: Spring, summer, and fall.

Environmental Conditions Needed: Prolonged rainy weather.

Spread By: Wind and splashing water.

Symptoms and Signs: The leaf blades and stolons are initially covered by a creamy white, slimy growth that quickly turns to a distinct purplish, ash-gray color—almost a sooty look. The impact can range from quite small to entire leaf blades, and covering several feet in diameter. The mold organism is not parasitizing or feeding on the grass leaves. It is saprophytic in nature, obtaining its nutrients from other sources. Any damage that may occur is from extended coverage for long periods of time, which excludes light, causing the leaf blades to yellow.

Can Resemble: Rust or powdery mildew early in its growth stage.

Management: Wipe off with a broom or cloth. Wash off with spray of water. Will stop with drier weather and frequent mowing.

Spring Dead Spot

Leptosphaeria spp.

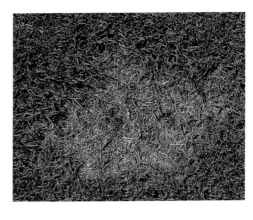

Grasses at Risk: Bermuda.

Season of Occurrence: Winter and early spring.

Environmental Conditions Needed: Air temperatures at low to mid 50s. Roots stimulated by late nitrogen feedings. More likely on lawns that are intensely managed.

Spread By: Soil movement on equipment and splashing soil.

Symptoms and Signs: Well-defined, circular spots occur as the lawn starts to green up in the spring. Dead patches of grass become evident with time. The dead areas can vary in size. Often identified as winter-kill. The leaves of the dead grass take on a straw color, and the rhizomes, stolons, and roots turn dark and appear rotted. The entire root and crown of the plants are killed. The disease affects the roots while the grass is dormant. Usually, the affected areas are green and healthy going into the winter, but as growth begins in the spring, the amount of damage becomes evident. The damage can vary from year to year, depending on the length and severity of the winter, overall moisture conditions, and the particular grass cultivar.

Can Resemble: Too early for most other problems. Distinctive pattern as well.

Management: Avoid late summer fertilizer applications after August in lawns prone to the disease. Consider more cold hardy cultivars of bermuda. Fungicide applications have not proven effective in control or prevention. If using a fungicide, apply in mid-September to mid-October as a drench in areas previously affected. Work dead areas with shovel, and fill back with healthy grass plugs. May have to do this on a yearly basis depending on severity of the problem. With time, the grass usually will grow back.

St. Augustine Decline Virus (SADV)

Panicum mosaic virus

Grasses at Risk: St. Augustine.

Season of Occurrence: Any time, but most noticeable in spring.

Environmental Conditions Needed: None in particular.

Spread By: Primarily by mechanical equipment such as rotary mowers, edgers, and weed eaters. Many viruses are also spread by insects with piercing-sucking mouth parts, although that has not been confirmed with St. Augustine decline virus to date.

Symptoms and Signs: SADV is a virus found in individual plant cells where it reproduces, spreading to other cells, eventually impeding the vigor of the plant. The symptoms are most obvious in the spring when grass tries to produce new shoots. Initially, there is light yellow mottling on individual blades. In subsequent years, the entire lawn declines, becomes stunted, and the leaves begin to yellow. The stolons are also stunted. Eventually the leaf blades die, killing small areas, then progressing across the entire lawn.

Can Resemble: Initially like downy mildew, possibly iron chlorosis.

Management: Avoid planting infected sod. Use resistant cultivars. Clean mowing equipment with a 10% chlorox solution after each use to help prevent spread of the virus.

Too Much Shade

Grasses at Risk: Any Southern lawn grass.

Season of Occurrence: During growing season.

Environmental Conditions Needed: Trees or buildings.

Spread By: Not applicable.

Symptoms and Signs: Grass begins to thin. Weeds increase. Higher risk of disease problems. And tree roots compete for water and nutrients.

Can Resemble: Nematodes, and most any pest problem.

Management: Raise the mowing height to the highest level. Use a sharp blade. Use more shade tolerant grasses. Overseed cool-season grasses regularly at the recommended time. Properly prune trees to allow more light. Convert to a perennial, shade-loving ground cover if the area is shaded more than six hours per day. A last resort is to choose between the tree and the lawn.

Table 3.1
Fertilizer Maintenance Programs

Turfgrass	Maintenance Level*	Total lbs. of actual nitrogen per 1000 sq. ft. per year**	Mar.	Apr.	Jun.	Aug.	Oct.
Bermudagrass	Low	1.0		1.0			
	Medium	2.0		1.0	1.0		
	High	3.0		1.0	1.0	1.0	
Carpetgrass	Low	1.0		1.0			
	Medium	2.0		1.0	1.0		
	High	3.0		1.0	1.0	1.0	
Centipedegrass	Low	0.5		0.5			
	Medium	1.0		0.5	0.5		
	High	2.0		1.0	1.0		
St. Augustinegrass	Low	1.0		1.0			
	Medium	2.0		1.0	1.0		
	High	3.0		1.0	1.0	1.0	
Zoysiagrass	Low	1.0		1.0			
	Medium	2.0		1.0	1.0		
	High	3.0		1.0	1.0	1.0	
Kentucky Bluegrass	Low	1.0	0.5				0.5
	Medium	2.0	1.0				1.0
	High	3.0	1.5				1.5
Tall Fescue	Low	1.0	0.5				0.5
	Medium	2.0	1.0				1.0
	High	3.0	1.5				1.5

*the maintenance level should be based upon professional soil test results

**see fertilizer conversion guidelines in the "how much to apply" section

***months of application can vary depending on your particular growing climate

Table 3.2

Common Organic Lawn Fertilizers and Analyses

Material*	% Nitrogen (NO_3 or NH_4)	%Phosphorus (P_2O_5)	%Potassium (K_2O)	Availability
Basic Slag[1]	-	8-11	-	slow-medium
Blood Meal	15.0	1.3	0.7	slow
Bone Meal	4.0	21.0	0.02	slow
Compost (unfortified)[2]	2.5	0.08	1.5	slow
Cottonseed Meal	7.0	1.3	1.2	slow
Dried Blood	12-15	3.0	-	medium-fast
Fish Emulsion	5.0	-	-	medium-fast
Fish Meal	8.0	7.0	-	slow
Greensand[3]	-	1.5	5.0	slow
Guano (bat manure)	12.0	-	-	medium
Hoof Meal/Horn Dust	12.5	1.8	-	slow
Kelp (seaweed)	1.7	0.8	5.0	slow
Leaves (pulverized)	0.9	0.2	0.3	slow
Manure (cattle)	2.0	1.0	2.0	medium
Manure (horse)	0.4	0.2	0.3	medium
Manure (poultry)	3-5	2-3	1-2	medium
Manure (sheep)	0.6	0.3	0.2	medium
Milorganite[4]	5.0	3.0	2.0	medium
Mushroom Compost	0.5	60.0	1.0	slow
Peat/Muck	2.0	0.5	0.8	slow
Soybean Meal	6.7	1.6	2.3	slow-medium
Wood Ashes	-	1-2	3-8	fast

*Nutrient analysis can vary widely depending on source and manufacturer

[1] Mineral by-product of the steel industry

[2] Unfortified means no synthetic or additional fertilizer was added during the composting process

[3] Mined under-sea deposits with many trace minerals

[4] Processed biomass microorganisms from sludge

Some organic sources attract wildlife that can dig in and damage your lawn

Table 3.3

Recommended Fertilizer Amounts

Fertilizer amounts to use per 1,000 square feet. Based on 1 pound of actual nitrogen
(actual N ÷ 100 = (z), then 1 ÷ (z) = amount per 1,000 square feet)
(example 22-0-0; 22 ÷ 100 = 0.22; 1 ÷ 0.22 = 4.545 or 5 pounds)

Fertilizer Blend Examples	Amount per 1,000 Square Feet
22-0-0	5.00 lbs.
33-0-0	3.00
45-0-0	2.20
10-20-10	10.00
13-13-13	7.69
16-4-8	6.25
17-17-17	5.88
18-46-0	5.55
11-48-0	9.09
13-0-44	7.69
0-0-60*	6.66
0-20-0*	20.00
0-45-0*	8.88

This list is not all encompassing. Choose the best ratio combination based on soil test results. The amounts applied can be rounded off.

*Phosphorus and potassium are based on 3-4 pounds P_2O_5 and K_2O per 1,000 square feet

(example 0-45-0; 45 ÷ 100 = 0.45; 4 ÷ 0.45 = 8.88 pounds P_2O_5/1000 square feet)

(example 0-0-60; 60 ÷ 100 = 0.60; 4 ÷ 0.60 = 6.66 pounds K_2O/1000 square feet)

Table 5.1

Perennial Ground Covers for Shade

Common Name	Other Name	Botanical Name	Cold Hardiness Zones	Comments
Ajuga	Bugleweed	Ajuga reptans	4-9	
Asiatic Jasmine	Confederate Jasmine	Trachelospermum jasminioides	7b-10	
Barren Strawberry		Waldsteinia ternata	6-10	
Barrenwort		Epimedium species	3-8	acidic soils
Bishop's Weed		Aegopodium podagraria	3-9	can be invasive
Bloodroot		Sanguinaria canadensis	4-8	
Bromeliads		Billbergia species	8-10	
Bunchberry		Cornus canadensis	2-6	sensitive to heat
Cast Iron Plant		Aspidistra elatior	8-10	
Coontie		Zamia integrifolia	8-10	
Creeping Charlie		Pilea nummulariifolia	7-10	can become lawn weed
Creeping Fig		Ficus species	8-10	
English Ivy		Hedera helix	4-9	can be invasive
Euonymus	Wintercreeper	Euonymus fortunei	5-9	can be invasive
Ferns		(assorted species)	4-9	
Foam Flower		Tiarella cordifolia	5-8	
Ginger		Asarum canadense	4-7	
Japanese Spurge	Pachysandra	Pachysandra terminalis	4-8	
Lamium	Archangel	Lamium maculatum	4-9	
Leadwort	Plumbago	Ceratostigma plumbaginoides	5-9	
Lilyturf	Monkey Grass	Liriope muscari	6-10	
Mazus		Mazus reptans	5-9	
Mondo Grass		Ophiopogon japonicus	6-10	
Moneywort	Creeping Jenny	Lysimachia nummularia	6-10	acidic soils
Moss		(numerous genera)		
Partridge Berry		Mitchella repens	8-10	acidic soils
Peacock Moss		Selaginella uncinata	6-10	
St. John's Wort		Hypericum calycinum	5-8	
Sweet Woodruff		Gallium odoratum	4-8	
Vinca	Periwinkle	Vinca minor/major	4-9	
Wedelia		Wedelia trilobata	8-10	
Woodland Phlox		Phlox stolonifera	3-8	
Wandering Jew		Tradescantia zebrina	8-10	

Table 5.2
Calculating Plant Quantities

Determine planting bed area: (width x length = square feet)

Recommended Spacing (inches, from center to center)	Number of Plants (per square foot)
6	4.00
8	2.25
10	1.44
12	1.00
18	0.44
24	0.25

Example: 125 sq. ft. bed with 10 in. spacing = 180 plants needed (1.44 × 125 sq. ft. = 180)

Table 5.3
Traffic Resistant Ground Covers

Common Name	Botanical Name	Light Preference	Cold Hardiness Zones	Foot-Traffic Tolerance
Baby's Tears	Soleirolia soleirolii	shade	9-10	moderate
Blue Moneywort	Lindernia grandiflora	part shade	7-10	moderate
Blue Star Creeper	Laurentia fluviatilis	part shade	5-10	heavy
Bronze Dutch Clover	Trifolium repens 'Autropurpureum'	part shade	4-9	moderate
Cinquefoil	Potentilla neumanniana	sun	5-9	heavy
Creeping Lobelia	Lobelia chinensis	part shade	7-10	moderate
Creeping Wire Vine	Muehlenbeckia axillaris	part shade	6-9	heavy
Dwarf Mondo Grass	Ophiopogon japonicus 'Nana'	part shade	7-10	moderate
Elfin Thyme	Thymus serphyllum 'Elfin'	sun, part shade	4-9	heavy
Irish Moss	Arenaria verna	part shade	4-9	heavy
Scotch Moss	Sagina subulata	part shade	4-9	heavy
Mazus	Mazus reptans	sun, part shade	4-9	moderate
Miniature Sedum	Sedum requieni	sun	5-9	heavy
Rupturewort	Herniaria glabra	sun	5-9	heavy
Scabwort	Raoulia australis	sun	7-9	heavy

Bermudagrass Cultivars

SEED AVAILABLE— (cultivars available as seed may also be sold as sod)

'Arizona Common'— poor cold hardiness and density

'Blackjack'

'Cheyenne'— forage type as well as lawn grass

'Continental'

'Guymon'— excellent cold hardiness

'Jackpot'

'Mirage'— good cold hardiness

'Mowhawk'— good cold hardiness

'NewMex Sahara'

'OKS 91-11'

'Paco Verde'

'Panama'— medium fine texture, dense cover

'Princess'— dense growth

'Quickstand'

'Savannah'

'Sonesta'

'Southern Star'

'Sundance'

'Sundevil'

'Sunstar'

'Sydney'— dense cover, fine texture

'Yukon'— excellent cold hardiness, spring dead spot tolerance, slow to establish

VEGETATIVE ONLY

'Baby'

'Bayshore'

'Everglades'

'Floradwarf'

'FloraTex'— many seed heads, low fertility and water requirements, some tolerance to dollar spot and bermuda mite

'Midfield'— good cold hardiness

'Midiron'— good cold hardiness (sometimes sold as **'EZ Turf'**)

'Midlawn'— good cold hardiness

'Midway'

'Mississippi Choice'

'Mississippi Express'

'Mississippi Pride'

'No Mow'— minimal seed

'Ormond'— early selection, poor cold hardiness, tolerant of leaf spot

'Santa Ana'— increased smog and salt tolerance

'Shanghai'

'Sunturf'

'Texturf 10'— sparse seed heads, medium texture, dark green color

'Tifeagle'— more cold hardy, dense growth

'Tifgreen' (Tifton 328)— widely used in South

'Tifsport'— non-preference to mole crickets

'Tifway' (Tifton 419)— widely used in South

'Tifway II'

'Tufcote' (a.k.a. Toughcoat)

'U-3'— widely used in South

'Uganda'

'Vamont'

Centipedegrass Cultivars

(Cultivars available as seed may also be sold as sod.)

'AU Centennial Dwarf' (AC-17)— vegetative only, semi-dwarf, and more tolerant of alkaline soils

'Georgia Common'— seed available

'Oklawn'— seed available, more tolerant of cold and drought

'Tennessee Hardy'— seed available, more cold tolerant

'Tennturf'— vegetative only, best cold tolerance to date

'Tifblair'— seed or vegetative, more cold tolerant, slightly faster growth rate

St. Augustinegrass Cultivars

(Most are available as sprigs, plugs, and sod.)

'Bitter Blue'— finer texture, more shade tolerant, but susceptible to chinch bug and SADV

'Common'— pasture type, very susceptible to chinch bug and other pests, marginal cold hardiness, poor lawn selection

'Delmar'— semi-dwarf selection with more cold and shade tolerance

'Floralawn'— marginal cold and shade tolerance, coarse texture, some resistance to SADV, chinch bug, sod webworm, and brown patch

'Floratam'— coarser, shade tolerant, some resistance to chinch bug and SADV

'Floratam II'— improved version of Floratam, with better cold tolerance

'Floratine'— finer texture, darker green, susceptible to chinch bug and SADV

'FX 10'— drought tolerant

'FX 33'

'Gulfstar'

'Jade'— semi-dwarf with more cold and shade tolerance, finer texture, susceptible to chinch bug, brown patch, and webworm

'Mercedes'

'Palmetto'— dwarf selection with more cold and shade tolerance

'Raleigh'— good cold and shade tolerance, some resistance to SADV but susceptible to chinch bug, iron deficiency common in alkaline soils

'Roselawn'— pasture type, susceptible to chinch bug and other pests, marginal cold hardiness, poor lawn selection

'Seville'— marginal cold tolerance, some resistance to SADV, semi-dwarf, more thatch prone

'Sunclipse'

'Texas Common'

Zoysiagrass Cultivars

(Available vegetatively unless otherwise noted.)

Zoysia japonica

'Belaire'— more shade and cold tolerant, susceptible to brown patch

'Cathay'

'Companion'— brand-name for improved Korean Common selection, coarser texture (available as seed)

'Crowne'— faster growth habit, coarser, and more cold tolerant

'El Toro'— faster growth, early green-up, rust tolerant, can use rotary mower

'Empress'— fine texture, more heat and humidity tolerant, dark color

'Empire'— fine texture, more heat and humidity tolerant, dark color

'Marquis'

'Meyer' (Z-52) (also sold as Amazoy)— improved drought and cold tolerance

'Midwest'— good cold tolerance but susceptible to brown patch

'Omni'

'Palisades'— faster coverage, more cold and salt tolerant

'Sunburst'

'Sunrise'— brand-name of improved Korean Common selection, coarser texture (available as seed)

'Zenith'— coarser (available as seed)

Z. matrella

'Cashmere'— finer texture, quicker growth, marginal cold tolerance

'Cavalier'— more shade tolerant, faster growth and finer texture, tolerant to armyworm

'Matrella'— common species

'Diamond'— more shade and salt tolerant, finer texture, good for gold courses, faster growing. poor cold tolerance

---

Z. sinica also called seashore grass, but is not the same as seashore paspalum, closely resembles *Zoysia japonica* but with better seed propagation and easier handling.

'J-14'

Hybrid (cross between two species of zoysia)

'Emerald' (Z. japonica × Z. matrella)— less cold tolerant

Kentucky Bluegrass Cultivars

(Available as seed or sod.)

'Amazon'

'America'

'Aspen'

'Blacksburg'

'Bluestar'

'Bristol'

'Chateau'

'Georgetown'

'Kentucky Blue'
  (a.k.a. Ken Blue)

'Liberty'

'Merit'

'Misty'

'Monopoly'

'Nassau'

'Nugget'

'Princeton'

'Reveille'— Texas-released cultivar with somewhat more heat and drought tolerance

'Suffolk'

'Sydesport'

'Touchdown'

'Wabash'

More adapted to southern conditions along transition zone between cool- and warm-season grasses:

'Adelphi'

'Baron'

'Glade'

'Midnight'

'Ram I'

'Vantage'

'Victa'

Tall Fescue Cultivars

(Available as seed and occasionally as sod.)

'Apache'

'Arid'

'Bonanza' (and improved selections)

'Coyote'

'Crewcut'

'Crossfire'

'Falcon'

'Finelawn'

'Houndog' (and improved selections)

'Jaguar'

'Monarch'

'Mustang'

'Olympic' (and improved selections)

'Phoenix'

'Rebel' (and improved selections)

'Rebel 3-D'

'Rebel Jr.'

'Southeast'— adapted to acid soils, drought tolerant, adapted to Southeast U.S.

'Titan'

'Tomahawk'

'Tribute'

'Twighlight'

(Cultivar lists are not all-inclusive.)

Weights, Measures, and Calculations for Lawn Care

Linear Measure:

12 inches = 1 foot	
3 feet = 1 yard	
5,280 feet = 1,760 yards or 1 mile	

Area Measure:

144 square inches = 1 square foot
9 square feet = 1 square yard or 1,296 square inches
1 acre = 43,560 square feet or 4,840 square yards
640 acres = 1 square mile

Cubic Measure:

Square feet times inches deep divided by 324 = cubic yards

1,728 cubic inches = 1 cubic foot	7.48 gallons = cubic foot
27 cubic feet = 1 cubic yard	2,150.42 cubic inches = 1 standard bushel
1 bushel = 1.25 cubic feet	231 cubic inches = 1 standard gallon (liquid)
1 cubic foot = 0.8 bushel	1 cubic foot = 7.48 gallons

Spreading bulk material like mulch or soil:

	3 Cubic Foot Bag	2 Cubic Foot Bag	1 Cubic Foot Bag
$1/2$ inch deep	covers 72 square feet	covers 48 square feet	covers 24 square feet
1 inch deep	covers 36 square feet	covers 24 square feet	covers 12 square feet
2 inches deep	covers 18 square feet	covers 12 square feet	covers 6 square feet
3 inches deep	covers 12 square feet	covers 8 square feet	covers 3 square feet

3 Cubic Foot Bag

Depth of Product	100 Square Feet	1,000 Square Feet
2 inches	6 bags	60 bags
3 inches	9 bags	90 bags
4 inches	11 bags	110 bags

2 Cubic Foot Bag

Depth of Product	100 Square Feet	1,000 Square Feet
2 inches	8 bags	80 bags
3 inches	12 bags	120 bags
4 inches	15 bags	150 bags

Weights, Measures, and Calculations for Lawn Care

Coverage in Square Feet	Square Feet	Inches Deep
1 cubic yard	1,944	$1/8$ inch
1 cubic yard	1,296	$1/4$ inch
1 cubic yard	648	$1/2$ inch
1 cubic yard	324	1 inch
1 cubic yard	162	2 inches
1 cubic yard	108	3 inches
1 cubic yard	81	4 inches
1 cubic yard	54	6 inches
1 cubic yard	40	8 inches
1 cubic yard	27	12 inches

Dry Measure:

2 pints = 1 quart (qt.)

(= 67.2006 cubic inches)

8 quarts = 1 peck (pk.)

(= 637.605 cubic inches or 16 pints)

4 pecks = 1 bushel (bu.)

(= 2550.4 cubic inches or 32 quarts)

1 (short) ton = 2,000 pound (lbs.)

1 (long) ton = 2,240 pounds (lbs.)

Liquid Measure:

Teaspoons (tsp.)

3 tsp. = 1 Tbs.

Tablespoons (Tbs.)

2 Tbs. = $1/8$ cup or 1 fluid ounces (fl. oz.)

4 Tbs. = $1/4$ cup or 1 fl. oz.

8 Tbs. = $1/2$ cup or $1/4$ pint

16 Tbs. = 1 cup or $1/2$ pint

Cups, pints, quarts

2 cups = 1 pint or 16 fl. oz.

2 pints = 1 quart

4 quarts = 1 gallon

Watering Your Lawn:

To cover 1,000 square feet with an inch of water takes 625 gallons

One gallon per minute (gpm) = 1,440 gallons per day

10.4 gallons per minute applies one inch of water over 1,000 square feet every hour

Gallons/minutes $\times$ 8.03 = cubic feet per hour

One gallon of water weighs 8.34 pounds

Weights, Measures, and Calculations for Lawn Care

More Conversions:

Multiply	To Obtain
bushels by 0.8	cubic feet
bushels by 0.04545	cubic yards
cubic feet by 1.2	bushels
cubic feet by 0.03704	cubic yards
cubic feet by 1728	cubic inches
cubic inches by 0.00002143	cubic yards
cubic inches by 0.0005787	cubic feet
cubic yards by 22	bushels
cubic yards by 27	cubic feet
cubic yards by 46.656	cubic inches
feet by 12	inches
feet by 1/3	yards
pounds by 16	ounces

Metric Conversions:

Area

1 square foot = 0.093 square meters	
1 square yard = 0.836 square meters	
1 acre = 4.047 square meters	
1 square mile=2.590 square kilometers	

Weight

1 pound = 0.454 kilograms
1 ton (short) = 0.907 metric tons
1 ton (long) = 1.016 metric tons

Volume

1 cubic foot = 0.028 cubic meters
1 cubic yard = 0.765 cubic meters

Capacity

1 quart (liquid) = 0.946 liters
1 quart (dry) = 1.101 liters
1 gallon (liquid) = 3.785 liters
1 bushel = 35.239 liters

Length

1 inch = 2.54 centimeters 1 yard = 0.924 meters
1 foot = 0.305 meters 1 mile = 1.609 kilometers

Glossary for Lawn Care

Acid soil: soil with a pH less than 7.0. The lower the pH the more acidic or "sour" the soil. Soils are acid when concentrations of bases like calcium and magnesium are low in relation to hydrogen and aluminum. This can occur naturally in forested areas or as a result of leached soils or growing crops. Sulfur is typically added to the soil to make it more acidic.

Aeration: the process of punching holes in the soil to increase the amount of oxygen available to plant roots and correct compaction problems.

Alkaline soil: soil with a pH greater than 7.0. The higher the pH the more alkaline or "sweet" the soil. Sometimes referred to as "basic" soil because it has high concentrations of bases as opposed to acids. Lime is typically added to the soil to make it more alkaline.

All-purpose fertilizer: powdered, liquid, or granular fertilizer with a balanced proportion of the three key nutrients—nitrogen (N), phosphorus (P), and potassium (K). It is suitable for maintenance nutrition for most plants.

Amendments: components added to soil to improve fertility or structure.

Annual: a plant that lives its entire life in one season. It is genetically determined to germinate, grow, flower, set seed, and die the same year. Some plants that are perennial in their native habitats, but not hardy in another region, such as tropical plants, can also be used as annuals.

Beneficial insects: insects or their larvae that prey on pest organisms and their eggs, or benefit the garden in another way. They may be flying insects, such as ladybugs, parasitic wasps, praying mantids, and soldier bugs, or soil dwellers such as predatory nematodes and ants. Spiders and earthworms are considered beneficial also although they are not technically insects.

Berm: soil raised above ground level to create height in the landscape or provide better drainage for a particular planting.

Broadleaved: plants having leaves of wider breadth in relation to length and thickness, in contrast to grassy plants. Broadleaved, or broadleaf, weeds are typically dicots, whereas grasses are monocots. Dicots and monocots respond differently to chemical controls.

Bt: abbreviation of *Bacillus thuringiensis*, an organism that attacks a certain stage in the life cycle of some pests. Forms of Bt can be created to target a particular species. Used as a natural pest control.

Canopy: the overhead branching area of a tree, usually referring to its extent including foliage.

Chlorotic: yellowing of leaves either from pest or nutrient problems.

Clumping: a contained growth habit versus a spreading growth habit.

Cold hardiness: the ability of a plant to survive the winter cold in a particular area.

Compaction: when soil particles are packed so tightly together that air and water cannot easily penetrate.

Complete fertilizer: containing all three major components of fertilizers— nitrogen (N), phosphorus (P), and potassium (K), although not necessarily in equal proportions. An incomplete fertilizer does not contain all three elements.

Compost: organic matter that has undergone progressive decomposition by microbial and macrobial activity until it is reduced to a spongy, fluffy texture. Added to soil of any type, it improves the soil's ability to hold air and water and to drain well.

Cool-season grass: turfgrasses that prefer and thrive in cooler northern conditions. They can remain green during milder winters.

Coring: the act of mechanically removing small plugs of soil from the ground, allowing for better penetration of oxygen and water to alleviate soil compaction, and also providing lodging places for new grass seed. Typically done in preparation for renewing an established lawn or installing a new one. Also called core aeration.

Crown: the base of a plant at, or just beneath, the surface of the soil where the roots meet the stems.

Cultivar: a CULTIvated VARiety. It is a naturally occurring form of a plant that has been identified as special or superior and is purposely selected for propagation and production.

Appendix

Deciduous plants: unlike evergreens, these trees and shrubs lose their leaves in the fall.

Desiccation: drying out of foliage tissues, usually due to drought or wind.

Dethatching: the process of raking or removing the mat of partially decomposed remnants of grass lodged at the soil surface, beneath the living grass layer. Can be done manually or mechanically; vertical mowing (or verticutting) is one method.

Dicot: shortening of the word "dicotyledon." Plant with two cotyledons or seed leaves emerging from its seed, such as a bean or an acorn.

Division: the practice of splitting apart plants to create several smaller-rooted segments. The practice is useful for controlling the plant's size and for creating more plants.

Dormancy or dormant period: time during which no growth occurs because of unfavorable environmental conditions. For some plants it is in winter, and for others summer. Many plants require this time as a resting period.

Drought tolerant: plants able to tolerate dry soil for varying periods of time. However, plants must first be well established before they are drought tolerant.

Established: the point at which a newly planted tree, shrub, flower, or grass begins to produce new growth, either foliage or stems. This is an indication that the roots have recovered from transplant shock and have begun to grow and spread.

Evergreen: plants that do not lose all of their foliage annually with the onset of winter. They do, however, shed older leaves at certain times of the year while retaining younger leaves, depending on the species.

Foliar: of or about foliage, usually referring to the practice of spraying foliage, as in fertilizing or treating with pesticide. Leaf tissues absorb liquid directly for fast results, and the soil is not affected.

Fungicide: a pesticide material for destroying or preventing fungus on plants.

Genus: a distinct botanical group within a family, typically containing several species. Plural form is "genera," referring to more than one genus.

Germinate: to sprout. Germination is a fertile seed's first stage of development.

Grading: changing the slope of the land, usually to make it more level or a more gradual incline.

Hardscape: the permanent, structural, non-plant part of a landscape, such as walls, sheds, pools, patios, arbors, and walkways.

Heat tolerance: the ability of a plant to withstand the summer heat in a particular area.

Herbaceous: plants having fleshy or soft stems, with very little woody tissue, as opposed to woody plants. Herbaceous and woody plant stems differ structurally, in that herbaceous plants undergo little or no secondary growth, while woody plants do.

Herbicide: a pesticide material for killing or preventing weeds.

Humus: partially decomposed organic matter.

Hybrid: a plant that is the result of intentional or natural cross-pollination between two or more plants of the same species or genus.

Insecticide: a pesticide material for killing, preventing, or protecting plants against harmful insects.

Integrated Pest Management: a combination of pest management techniques used in order to reduce the need for pesticides. Also referred to by the acronym IPM.

Invasive: when a plant has such a vigorous growth habit that it crowds out more desirable plants.

Irrigation: manmade systems of pipes, sprinkler heads, and timers installed to provide supplementary water to landscaping.

Leaching: the removal of nutrients from the soil by excessive amounts of water.

Life cycle: stages in the life of an organism. With insects it is important to know the cycles of both beneficial and harmful ones, since different stages vary in their locations, vulnerabilities, and eating habits.

Micronutrients: elements needed in small quantities for plant growth. Sometimes a soil will be deficient in one or more of them and require a particular fertilizer formulation.

Monocot: shortening of the word "monocotyledon." Plant with one cotyledon or seed leaf emerging from its seed, such as with corn or grass.

Mowing strip: a type of barrier placed between the lawn and landscaped areas that accommodates lawnmower tires, making it easier to mow the lawn edge neatly, and preventing ruts or compaction to the edges of the beds.

Mulch: a layer of material over bare soil to protect it from erosion and compaction, and for moisture retention, temperature control, weed prevention, and aesthetics.

Mulching mower: mower that chops grass blades into very fine pieces, eliminating the need to have an attachment that bags the clippings.

Node: structure on a stem from which leaves, roots, and branches arise.

Non-selective: herbicides that have the potential to kill or control any plant to which they are applied.

Nutrients: elements available through soil, air, and water, which the plant utilizes for growth and reproduction.

Organic material, organic matter: any material or debris that is derived from living things. It is carbon-based material capable of undergoing decomposition and decay.

Overseeding: distributing new grass seed on an established lawn to thicken the grass coverage or introduce another type of grass to extend green season.

Partial shade: situation with filtered or dappled sunlight, or half a day of shade. In the South, part shade often refers to afternoon shade, when the sun is at its brightest and hottest.

Pathogen: the causal organism of a plant disease.

Peat moss: organic matter from peat sedges (United States) or sphagnum mosses (Canada), often used to improve soil texture. The acidity of sphagnum peat moss makes it ideal for boosting or maintaining soil acidity while also improving its drainage.

Perennial: a plant that lives over two or more seasons. Many die back with frost, but its roots survive the winter and generate new shoots in the spring.

pH: a measurement of the relative acidity (low pH) or alkalinity (high pH) of soil or water based on a scale of 1 to 14, 7 being neutral. Individual plants require soil to be within a certain range so that nutrients can dissolve in moisture and be available to them.

Plug: piece of sod used in establishing a new lawn. Plugs can also be grown or purchased in small cells or pots within a flat, sometimes referred to as trays.

Pollen: the yellow, powdery grains in a flower. A plant's male sex cells, they are transferred to the female plant parts by means of wind or animal pollinators to fertilize them and create seeds.

Pre-emergent: an herbicide applied to the soil surface to prevent weed seed from germinating.

Post-emergent: an herbicide applied to already germinated and actively growing weeds to kill or control them.

Reel mower: type of mower generally thought of as old fashioned, but with new versions achieving renewed popularity. Blades are arranged horizontally in a cylinder, or reel, that spins, cutting the grass blades against a metal plate.

Renovation: renewing an established lawn, partially or completely.

Rhizome: a swollen energy-storing stem structure, that lies horizontally in the soil, with roots emerging from its lower surface and growth shoots from a growing point at or near its tip, as in bermudagrass.

Rotary mower: a mower with its blades arranged under the body of the mower, which cuts by the high speed of the spinning blades.

Runner: horizontal stem that grows along the soil surface and forms plantlets at each node. An example is the strawberry.

Runoff: when water moves across the landscape without being absorbed, because the slope is steep, the volume of water is greater than the absorption capacity of the soil, the soil is compacted, or the surface is of an impenetrable material. Runoff from areas that have had chemicals applied can cause problems in the areas ultimately receiving the water.

Selection: a variation within a species that occurs naturally due to the presence of a multitude of genetic possibilities. Over several generations plants with the desired characteristic are isolated and propagated. This process has been particularly important in the agronomic industry.

Selective: herbicides, and other pesticides, that target a particular type of weed or pest.

Self-seeding: the tendency of some plants to sow their seeds freely around the yard. Can create many seedlings the following season that may or may not be welcome.

Semi-evergreen: tending to be evergreen in a mild climate but deciduous in a rigorous one.

Shade tolerant: a plant's ability to maintain health and continue growth in a shaded location.

Slow-acting fertilizer: fertilizer that is insoluble in water, designated as slow release or controlled release, and releases its nutrients gradually as a function of soil temperature, moisture, and related microbial activity. Typically granular, it may be organic or synthetic.

Sod: commercially grown turfgrass sections cut from a field in rectangular panels or rolls, used to establish new lawns.

Soil conditioner: chemical or organic material which aggregates soil particles for improved structure.

Species: a group of fundamentally identical plants within a genus. Synonymous with the more botanically accurate designation "specific epithet."

Sprig: part of an underground root or stem that contains nodes, used to establish new plants.

Sterile: producing no viable seeds or spores, and in lawn grasses no flowers, which is an advantage since the flowers are typically taller than the leaf blades and are not attractive. The disadvantage is that such grasses cannot be bought as seed, only as sod.

Stolon: horizontal stem that grows along the soil surface. It can form plantlets at the tips of the stems. An example is the blackberry.

Synthetic: products made to imitate a natural material, as in synthetic fertilizer or pesticide.

Tamp: pressing down on newly installed sod so that the roots have good soil contact. This can also be achieved with "rolling," in which a heavy cylindrical drum is rolled over the sod.

Thatch: layer of undecayed grass found between the soil surface and the living grass blades.

Threshold: the level at which a pest becomes harmful to its target host plant. Lower levels of the pest might not be harmful.

Topdressing: the act of applying granular products such as fertilizer, lime, sand, etc. over the top of lawn grass.

Topsoil: the fertile layer of soil where plant roots grow. Sometimes the naturally occurring topsoil is inadequate for certain plants, or has been removed during construction, in which case it might be necessary to purchase topsoil from a local supplier.

Translocation: movement of water, minerals, and food within the plant.

Transpiration: water loss by evaporation from external leaf surfaces.

Transplanting: moving plants from one location to another.

Turf or turfgrass: grass used to make a lawn.

Turfscaping: wise use of turf in the overall landscape.

Variety: a group of plants within a species which have stable characteristics separating them from the typical form. Frequently used synonymously with cultivar and selection, even though there are differences in the definitions of the three terms.

Vegetative: non-sexual production of plant material typically achieved by divisions or cuttings and not as a result of flowering, pollination, and seed formation.

Vertical mowing or verticutting: mechanical act of cutting into a lawn vertically with sharp blades or tines to lift dead vegetation such as thatch.

Viability: refers to seed that is healthy and able to germinate.

Warm-season grass: turfgrasses that thrive and perform in warm southern conditions. They can go dormant during the coldest parts of the winter, then resume growth in the spring.

Water-logged: soil that holds too much water for most plants to thrive, associated with poor aeration, inadequate drainage, or soil compaction.

Weed: a plant growing where it is not wanted.

Weed-and-feed: a product that combines a weed control, usually pre-emergent, and a fertilizer. Timing of an application is critical since a pre-emergent weed control is also capable of preventing grass seed from germinating, and fertilizing before the grass is actively growing might actually promote the growth of existing weeds.

White grubs: fat, off-white, wormlike larvae of beetles. They reside in the soil and many types feed on plant (especially grass) roots until later in the season when they emerge as beetles.

Bibliography

Bost, Toby. *North Carolina Gardener's Guide*. Franklin, TN: Cool Springs Press. 1997.

Boyd, John, and Mike Richardson. *Zoysia japonica From Sprigs: Effects of Topdressing and Nitrogen Fertility*. University of Arkansas, HortScience 36(2): 377-379. 2001.

Duble, Richard. *Identifying Turf Problems*. Florida Turf Digest. Vol. 3, No. 9, 1986.

Gill, Dan and Joe White. *Louisiana Gardener's Guide*. Franklin, TN: Cool Springs Press. 1997.

Glasener, Erica and Walter Reeves. *Georgia Gardener's Guide*. Franklin, TN: Cool Springs Press. 1996.

Greer, Jennifer. *Alabama Gardener's Guide*. Franklin, TN: Cool Springs Press. 1997.

Groom, Dale. *Texas Gardening Guide*. Franklin, TN: Cool Springs Press. 1997.

Martin, Glen. Oklahoma Turfgrass Survey. Stillwater, OK: OSU. 1987.

Murphy, Tim R. and et al. *Weeds of Southern Turfgrasses*. Gainesville, FL: University of Florida Cooperative Extension Service, Institute of Food and Agricultural Sciences.

NeSmith, J. and E.W. McElwee. *Soil Reaction (pH) for Flowers, Shrubs, and Lawn*. Circular 352-A. Gainesville, FL: Florida Cooperative Extension Service IFAS, 1974.

Tucker, Billy and et al. *Oklahoma Soil Fertility Handbook*. Stillwater, OK: Oklahoma Cooperative Extension Service, 1977.

Unknown. *Grounds Maintenance* 36(8). Research Update, Sharp Blades Conserve Fuel. Overland Park, KS: August 2001.

Wilson, Jim. *South Carolina Gardener's Guide*. Franklin, TN: Cool Springs Press. 1997.

Winter, Norman. *Mississippi Gardener's Guide*. Franklin, TN: Cool Springs Press. 2000.

Zak, Bill. *Florida Critters*. Dallas, TX: Taylor Publishing Co., 1986.

Photography Credits

Index

Meet the Author

Steve Dobbs is an award-winning horticulturist, garden writer, and lecturer. He was host and producer of the popular television show "Oklahoma Gardening" from 1990 to 1995, which was selected as the Best TV Gardening Program in the Nation by the Garden Writers Association of America in 1992.

Since his graduation from Oklahoma State University and the University of Arkansas in Horticulture, Steve has worked in a wide variety of horticulture-related fields, including the retail and wholesale nursery trade; landscape design, installation, and maintenance; and in education as an Extension Horticulturist in both Oklahoma and Florida. For fourteen years he worked with volunteers through the Cooperative Extension Service, equipping gardeners to better answer questions and solve horticulture problems.

Among Steve's previous publications is the *Oklahoma Gardener's Guide*. He has also written gardening columns for various papers in Oklahoma, Florida, Texas, and Arkansas.

When Steve is not busy taking care of over 40 acres of bermuda, zoysia, and fescue turfgrasses as Director of Landscape and Grounds for the University of Arkansas, Fort Smith, he can be found tending his own $1^1/4$ acre bermudagrass lawn at his farm in eastern Oklahoma.